# Beating China: A Blueprint for American Victory

Dr. Alain Dupet

Published by Dr. Alain Dupet, 2025.

While every precaution has been taken in the preparation of this book, the publisher assumes no responsibility for errors or omissions, or for damages resulting from the use of the information contained herein.

BEATING CHINA: A BLUEPRINT FOR AMERICAN VICTORY

**First edition. January 26, 2025.**

Copyright © 2025 Dr. Alain Dupet.

ISBN: 979-8230669500

Written by Dr. Alain Dupet.

# Table of Contents

Table of Contents .................................................................. 1

# Table of Contents

Introduction

Part 1 – Understanding the Chinese Challenge

Chapter 1 – The Chinese Communist Party's (CCP) Strategic Blueprint

Chapter 2 – China's Economic and Technological Powerhouse

Chapter 3 – Assessing China's Vulnerabilities

Part 2 – America's Strengths and Strategies

Chapter 4 – Unleashing American Innovation

Chapter 5 – Building a Resilient Economy

Chapter 6 – Forging Stronger Alliances

Chapter 7 – Countering Aggression and Promoting Freedom

Part 3 – Implementing the Winning Strategy

Chapter 8 – Reforming Government and Mobilizing Resources

Chapter 9 – Winning the Information War

Chapter 10 – Securing America's Future

Conclusion

## Introduction

The 21st century has witnessed the rise of China as a formidable global power. Fueled by decades of rapid industrialization and a focus on export-driven growth, China's economic ascent has been meteoric, transforming it from a peripheral player to a major force on the world stage. This dramatic transformation has fundamentally reshaped the geopolitical landscape, ushering in a new era of intense competition with the United States.

This rivalry extends far beyond traditional military confrontation, encompassing a multifaceted struggle across a wide range of domains. Economic competition is fierce, with both nations vying for technological dominance in critical sectors like artificial intelligence, 5G, biotechnology, and semiconductors. China's ambitious "Made in China 2025" initiative, aimed at achieving global leadership in advanced manufacturing, poses a direct challenge to American technological supremacy. This economic competition is further complicated by issues of intellectual property theft, cyberespionage, and concerns about the security of Chinese technology, particularly in areas like telecommunications infrastructure.

Geopolitical competition is also intensifying. China's growing global influence is evident in initiatives like the Belt and Road Initiative, a massive infrastructure development project spanning continents that is expanding China's economic and political reach across Asia, Africa, and Europe. This initiative, coupled with China's assertive military posturing in the South

China Sea, including its construction of artificial islands and military installations, is altering the regional balance of forces and raising concerns about freedom of navigation in crucial waterways.

Beyond economic and geopolitical competition, the US-China rivalry reflects a clash of ideologies. China's authoritarian model of governance, characterized by state control over the economy and suppression of dissent, stands in stark contrast to the democratic values and principles championed by the United States. This ideological competition manifests in various ways, including competition for influence in international organizations, efforts to shape global narratives through state-sponsored media outlets and propaganda campaigns, and struggles over the future direction of international norms and standards.

The stakes in this rivalry are immense. The outcome will determine the global balance of power, the future of the international order, and the prosperity and security of countless individuals around the world. The United States must develop a comprehensive and nuanced strategy to navigate this complex and challenging relationship, ensuring that American interests and values are protected and promoted in a rapidly changing world. This will require a multi-pronged approach that addresses the challenges of economic competition, geopolitical rivalry, and ideological differences while also seeking areas of potential cooperation where mutual interests align.

The US-China strategic competition transcends traditional geopolitical rivalry, evolving into a multifaceted struggle across a spectrum of domains. At its core lies a systemic clash between two competing models for global order: the US-led liberal international order, founded on principles of democracy, open markets, and multilateral cooperation, and China's emerging alternative, characterized by authoritarian governance, state-led economic development, and a more assertive, revisionist foreign policy.

Furthermore, both countries are engaged in sophisticated information and influence operations. These operations involve the use of cyberattacks, disinformation campaigns, and the exploitation of social media platforms to shape global perceptions, manipulate public opinion, and advance their respective narratives. This includes the spread of misinformation, the targeting of critical infrastructure, and the interference in foreign elections.

This competition is not merely a series of isolated incidents but rather a long-term strategic endeavor with significant implications for the global order. It is characterized by increasing complexity and the potential for unintended consequences, such as an arms race, economic decoupling, and even military conflict. Navigating this challenging relationship requires careful consideration, a focus on mitigating risks, and a commitment to finding areas of cooperation where mutual interests align.

The 21st century is witnessing a dramatic shift in global power dynamics, characterized by the rise of new actors and the decline of traditional Western dominance. This shift is fundamentally altering the international order, eroding the foundations of the rules-based system that has underpinned global cooperation for decades.

The rise of China as a major economic and military power is arguably the most significant factor driving these changes. China's rapid economic growth, fueled by decades of sustained development and innovation, has propelled it to become the world's second-largest economy, challenging US economic hegemony. This economic ascendancy has translated into growing political and military influence on the global stage. China's assertive foreign policy, including its military expansion in the South China Sea, its Belt and Road Initiative aimed at expanding its global infrastructure and influence, and its increasing technological prowess in areas like artificial intelligence and 5G, are altering the geopolitical landscape and challenging the existing balance of power.

Furthermore, the resurgence of great power competition, exemplified by the rivalry between the United States and China, is straining existing alliances and creating new fault lines in international relations. This competition is not merely economic and military but also ideological, with differing visions for the future of the international order. The United States champions a liberal international order based on democracy, human rights, and multilateralism, while China promotes an alternative model of authoritarian governance and state-centric international relations.

The erosion of the rules-based international order is evident in several key areas. Multilateral institutions, such as the United Nations and the World Trade Organization, are facing increasing challenges to their authority and effectiveness. The rise of nationalism and populism in many countries, coupled with the growing influence of illiberal regimes, is undermining support for international cooperation and contributing to a more inward-looking and protectionist global environment. This is evident in the increasing use of unilateralism, the withdrawal of countries from international agreements, and the erosion of trust in international institutions.

The breakdown of trust and the proliferation of disinformation are further eroding the foundations of the international order. The spread of misinformation and the manipulation of information through social media platforms are undermining public discourse, eroding trust in traditional sources of information, and making it more difficult to achieve common ground on global challenges. This "infodemic" exacerbates existing divisions, fuels xenophobia and intolerance, and hinders effective international cooperation on issues such as climate change, pandemics, and global security.

The consequences of this erosion are significant. The decline of the rules-based order could lead to increased instability, conflict, and uncertainty in the international system. It could also undermine efforts to address global challenges such as climate change, pandemics, and poverty, which require international cooperation and collective action. The potential for miscalculation and escalation of tensions between major powers is a growing concern, while the erosion of international norms could embolden authoritarian regimes and weaken the protection of human rights.

Addressing these challenges requires a multifaceted approach. This includes strengthening existing multilateral institutions, promoting dialogue and cooperation among major powers, and reaffirming the importance of international law and norms. It also requires addressing the root causes of global instability, such as poverty, inequality, and climate change, and promoting inclusive and sustainable development. Furthermore, combating the spread of disinformation and strengthening democratic institutions are crucial for restoring trust and ensuring the long-term viability of the international order.

The Indo-Pacific region, particularly the South China Sea, Taiwan, and the Philippines, has emerged as a critical geopolitical theater in the 21st century, shaping the global balance of power and driving major strategic competition between the United States and China. These areas are fraught with tensions, driven by competing territorial claims, strategic interests, and ideological differences that have the potential to escalate into major conflicts with global ramifications.

The South China Sea, with its rich fishing grounds, potential hydrocarbon reserves, and vital shipping lanes, has become a major flashpoint. China's expansive claims over nearly the entire sea, based on a historical interpretation known as the "nine-dash line," have sparked territorial disputes with several Southeast Asian nations, including Vietnam, the Philippines, and Malaysia. China has aggressively asserted its claims through large-scale island construction, militarization of artificial reefs, and assertive maritime activities, such as close encounters with vessels from other claimants, leading to increased tensions and a heightened risk of military confrontation. These actions have challenged the freedom of navigation and overflight in this crucial waterway, a principle vital for global trade and regional stability.

The Taiwan Strait is another major source of geopolitical tension. China views Taiwan as an integral part of its territory, while Taiwan maintains its own democratic system and de facto independence. The possibility of China using force to reunify Taiwan with the mainland remains a significant threat to regional and global stability. Any conflict over Taiwan would have profound economic and security implications, potentially triggering a wider regional and even global conflict. This scenario would disrupt global supply chains, impact global trade, and potentially escalate into a major power confrontation with unpredictable consequences.

The Philippines, strategically located in Southeast Asia, plays a crucial role in regional security. As a key US ally, the Philippines provides vital access to military bases, allowing the United States to project power in the region and counter China's growing influence. The Enhanced Defense Cooperation Agreement between the two countries allows for increased US military presence in the Philippines, enhancing regional security cooperation. However, the Philippines also faces internal security challenges, including insurgencies and terrorism, which further complicate its strategic environment and require careful balancing of domestic and foreign policy priorities.

The geopolitical significance of these regions lies in their strategic importance to global trade, energy security, and regional stability. The South China Sea is a crucial maritime passage for global trade, with trillions of dollars worth of goods passing through its waters annually. Any disruption to freedom of navigation in the South China Sea, whether through military confrontation, accidents, or unilateral actions by any claimant, would have severe economic consequences for the global economy.

Furthermore, these regions are central to the ongoing competition between the United States and China. The US seeks to maintain its influence in the Indo-Pacific, uphold a rules-based international order, and ensure freedom of navigation and overflight. China seeks to expand its regional and global power, challenge the existing US-led order, and establish its dominance in the region. This competition has led to increased military activity, including naval exercises, arms races, and the development of advanced military capabilities, such as hypersonic weapons and cyber warfare, raising the stakes and increasing the risk of miscalculation and escalation.

In conclusion, the Indo-Pacific region, particularly the South China Sea, Taiwan, and the Philippines, is a critical geopolitical theater with significant implications for global security and prosperity. Understanding the complex dynamics at play in these regions, including the competing territorial claims, strategic interests, and ideological differences, is crucial for navigating the challenges of the 21st century and ensuring peace and stability in the Asia-Pacific. This requires diplomatic efforts to resolve disputes peacefully, strengthen regional cooperation, and uphold a rules-based international order that ensures freedom of navigation, peaceful resolution of disputes, and respect for international law.

The Panama Canal, a marvel of engineering connecting the Atlantic and Pacific Oceans, stands as a crucial artery for international trade. Operated by the Panama Canal Authority (ACP), an independent agency of the Panamanian government, the canal significantly reduces shipping times and costs, facilitating commerce between the Americas, Asia, and Europe. By dramatically shortening maritime routes, it drives economic growth and reduces transportation costs. The canal's impact on global supply chains is undeniable, with a significant portion of global trade, including vital commodities and manufactured goods, traversing its waters.

The Caribbean Basin, encompassing the Caribbean Sea and its surrounding islands and coastlines, further amplifies this strategic importance. This region boasts crucial maritime routes, serving as a major conduit for trade and energy transport, including a substantial portion of US oil imports. Its proximity to the United States adds another layer of strategic value, making it a region of vital interest for US national security.

However, the Caribbean Basin faces a confluence of challenges with significant geopolitical implications. Drug trafficking remains a major issue, fueling violence, corruption, and instability. This not only destabilizes individual countries but also poses security threats to the entire hemisphere, impacting drug markets and fueling transnational criminal organizations. Natural disasters, such as hurricanes and earthquakes, frequently batter the region, causing widespread devastation and humanitarian crises. These events exacerbate existing social and economic vulnerabilities, hindering development and requiring significant international assistance for recovery and reconstruction. Climate change poses significant threats, including rising sea levels, more frequent and intense hurricanes, and coral reef degradation. These environmental challenges threaten coastal communities, vital tourism sectors, and the region's overall economic stability. Political instability, social unrest, and internal conflicts are prevalent in some parts of the region, contributing to instability and hindering economic development. These challenges can create power vacuums that can be exploited by external actors and exacerbate regional tensions.

Furthermore, the growing competition between the United States and China adds another layer of complexity to the geopolitical landscape. China has been actively expanding its economic and political influence in the region through initiatives such as the Belt and Road Initiative, investing in infrastructure projects and key sectors. This increased Chinese presence raises concerns about potential security challenges, competition for influence, and the potential for debt traps for some Caribbean nations.

The geopolitical significance of the Panama Canal and the Caribbean Basin demands close attention from regional and international actors. Addressing the multifaceted challenges facing the region, including combating drug trafficking, mitigating the impacts of climate change, promoting political stability, and fostering sustainable economic development, is crucial. These efforts are essential for maintaining regional stability, ensuring the continued flow of global trade through this vital corridor, and safeguarding the economic and security interests of all stakeholders. This analysis underscores the critical importance of the Panama Canal and the Caribbean Basin in the contemporary global context, highlighting the interconnectedness of these regions and the multifaceted challenges that must be addressed to ensure their continued stability and prosperity.

Donald Trump began his second term as the 47th president of the United States of America in January 2025 and brought Elon Musk on board. Elon Musk, a titan of the technology and automotive industries, occupies a unique and complex position within the escalating US-China competition. As the CEO of Tesla, a leading electric vehicle manufacturer with significant operations in China, Musk navigates a delicate balance between the demands of his business and the broader geopolitical landscape.

Tesla's success in China is undeniable. The Chinese market has been crucial for the company's growth, providing access to a vast consumer base and a robust supply chain. Tesla has established a significant manufacturing presence in Shanghai, contributing to its global production and sales. This reliance on the Chinese market, however, has drawn considerable scrutiny. Critics argue that Tesla's operations in China could potentially compromise US technological advantages, raising concerns about the transfer of sensitive data and intellectual property. Moreover, the Chinese government's increasing influence over the business environment in China raises questions about the company's autonomy and its ability to operate independently of Beijing's interests.

Despite these concerns, Musk has consistently advocated for closer economic ties with China. He has publicly emphasized the importance of global cooperation, particularly in addressing critical challenges such as climate change, arguing that a confrontational approach with China would be detrimental to global progress. He has also sought to position Tesla as a bridge between the two countries, fostering technological exchange and promoting economic interdependence. This stance has positioned him as an unconventional voice in the ongoing debate about US-China relations, often diverging from the more cautious and competitive approach favored by many US policymakers.

However, Musk's stance on various geopolitical issues, including Taiwan and the war in Ukraine, has frequently diverged from prevailing US government policy, leading to criticism and raising concerns about potential conflicts of interest. His comments on these issues have often been perceived as sympathetic to China's position, further complicating his relationship with the US government and raising questions about his loyalty and commitment to US national interests.

Musk's actions and statements have made him a central figure in the ongoing debate about the nature of US-China relations, the role of technology in geopolitical competition, and the challenges of balancing economic interests with national security concerns. His case highlights the complexities of navigating the evolving global landscape, where economic interdependence is intertwined with geopolitical rivalry. As Tesla continues to grow and expand its global footprint, Musk will undoubtedly continue to face these challenges, navigating the delicate tightrope between business success and the broader geopolitical implications of his actions.

Elon Musk is undeniably a driving force of innovation across various sectors, pushing the boundaries of technology and inspiring a new era of exploration. His contributions to the automotive industry and space exploration are significant and far-reaching, leaving an indelible mark on both fields.

In the automotive industry, Musk revolutionized electric vehicles through Tesla. He challenged the conventional wisdom of the automotive industry by spearheading the development of high-performance, long-range electric cars that were not only environmentally friendly but also desirable and technologically advanced. Tesla's innovations, such as advancements in battery technology, the development of sophisticated autopilot systems, and the integration of cutting-edge software, have significantly impacted the entire automotive industry. Tesla's success has forced traditional automakers to accelerate their own electric vehicle programs, leading to increased competition and ultimately accelerating the transition to sustainable transportation.

Musk's impact on space exploration through SpaceX is equally profound. SpaceX has revolutionized space transportation by developing and successfully implementing reusable rockets. This breakthrough has dramatically reduced the cost of launching payloads into orbit, making space travel more accessible and affordable. SpaceX has not only successfully launched and landed numerous rockets, demonstrating remarkable engineering feats, but has also expanded access to space for both commercial and government entities. Furthermore, SpaceX's ambitious projects, such as the development of the Starship spacecraft, aim to facilitate human exploration of Mars, a goal that once seemed purely within the realm of science fiction. These ambitious projects are pushing the boundaries of space technology and inspiring a new generation of engineers and scientists.

Beyond his specific achievements in these fields, Musk's leadership style and his ability to inspire and motivate teams of engineers and scientists are equally noteworthy. He fosters a culture of innovation and encourages ambitious, even seemingly impossible, goals. His unwavering belief in the potential of technology and his willingness to challenge conventional wisdom have not only disrupted existing markets but have also paved the way for future advancements in technology and space exploration.

Musk's contributions to technology and space exploration have solidified his place as a visionary leader and a prominent figure in shaping the future of humanity. His companies have not only disrupted existing markets but have also inspired a new era of innovation and exploration, pushing the boundaries of what is possible and inspiring generations to come.

Elon Musk's companies, particularly Tesla and SpaceX, are deeply intertwined with the evolving US-China competition. Tesla's advancements in electric vehicle technology, including cutting-edge battery technology, sophisticated autonomous driving software, and innovative vehicle design, have the potential to solidify US technological leadership in this crucial sector. By maintaining a competitive edge in areas like battery production and artificial intelligence for autonomous driving, the US can strengthen its position in the global electric vehicle market and ensure long-term economic and strategic advantage. SpaceX, through its development of reusable rockets, advanced launch systems, and ambitious projects like Starship, is pushing the boundaries of space exploration and positioning the US at the forefront of space technology. This technological dominance is crucial for maintaining US military and strategic advantage in space, an increasingly contested domain. Tesla's global success, including its significant operations in China, contributes significantly to US economic growth and job creation. The company employs thousands of workers in the US across its manufacturing, research and development, and sales and service operations. SpaceX is also a major employer, creating high-skilled jobs in engineering, manufacturing, and other related fields. Furthermore, SpaceX's commercial space ventures, such as Starlink, have the potential to generate significant revenue and create new economic opportunities across various sectors. SpaceX's international collaborations on space projects, such as launching satellites for other countries, can foster international cooperation and potentially build bridges with other nations, including potential competitors like China. These collaborations can create avenues for dialogue and cooperation on issues of mutual interest, such as space debris mitigation and the peaceful exploration of space. However, Tesla's operations in China raise significant concerns about the potential transfer of sensitive technology and intellectual property to Chinese competitors. This includes concerns about the theft of trade secrets, the forced transfer of technology, and the potential for Chinese government influence over the company's operations. Tesla's reliance on the Chinese market for production and sales creates a degree of dependency on China, which could be leveraged for political or economic advantage. This dependence could expose Tesla to potential risks, such as government regulations, trade restrictions, or even nationalization, which could significantly impact the company's operations and profitability. While SpaceX can contribute to US space dominance, its activities could also intensify space-based competition with China. The development of advanced space technologies, such as satellite constellations for military and intelligence purposes, could increase the risk of conflict in this domain. Neuralink's brain-computer interface technology, while potentially revolutionary, also raises significant ethical and national security concerns. The potential for misuse of this technology, particularly by foreign adversaries, requires careful consideration and appropriate safeguards. Elon Musk's companies, particularly Tesla and SpaceX, are deeply intertwined with the evolving US-China competition, presenting a unique blend of opportunities and significant risks. Navigating these complexities requires a nuanced approach that balances the need for technological innovation and economic growth with the imperative of safeguarding US national security and strategic interests. This will require careful consideration of the potential benefits and drawbacks of Musk's companies' activities within the broader context of US-China relations, including developing appropriate safeguards to mitigate the risks associated with technology transfer, maintaining a diverse and resilient supply chain, and ensuring responsible development and deployment of emerging technologies.

China's ascent as a global power is arguably the most significant geopolitical development of the 21st century. Fueled by decades of sustained economic growth, China has emerged as a major economic and military force, fundamentally altering the global balance of power and challenging the existing international order.

Economically, China's rise has been nothing short of spectacular. It has experienced unprecedented growth, becoming the world's second-largest economy, surpassing many developed nations in terms of GDP. This economic growth is underpinned by its manufacturing prowess, transforming China into the world's factory. Chinese manufacturing dominates key industries such as technology, manufacturing, and renewable energy, with "Made in China" products ubiquitous in global markets. China's Belt and Road Initiative (BRI), a massive infrastructure development project spanning continents, has further amplified its economic influence. The BRI aims to connect Asia with Europe and Africa through a network of roads, railways, ports, and other infrastructure projects, expanding China's economic reach and deepening its political and economic ties with numerous countries across the globe.

This remarkable economic growth has translated into significant military modernization. China has invested heavily in its military, transforming the People's Liberation Army (PLA) into a modern, technologically advanced fighting force. The PLA has modernized its arsenal with advanced weaponry, including aircraft carriers, stealth fighters, long-range missiles, and cyberwarfare capabilities. The PLA Navy has expanded its global reach, conducting naval exercises and deployments in distant waters, projecting Chinese power beyond its immediate region.

China's growing economic and military power has profound implications for the global order. It directly challenges US global dominance, leading to increased competition in various domains, including technology, trade, and military influence. Trade disputes have become increasingly frequent, with both sides imposing tariffs and restrictions on each other's goods. Moreover, the military competition between the two powers is escalating, with increased naval activity in the South China Sea and concerns about the potential for conflict in the Taiwan Strait.

The rise of China presents both opportunities and challenges for other countries. While China's economic growth has benefited many countries through trade and investment, it also poses challenges, such as increased competition and concerns about economic dependence. Many countries are now navigating a complex geopolitical landscape, seeking to balance their relationships with both the US and China while safeguarding their own national interests.

China's continued ascent will undoubtedly shape the 21st century. The nature of the US-China relationship will have a profound impact on global stability and prosperity. Managing this competition effectively will require diplomacy, cooperation, and a clear-eyed assessment of the challenges and opportunities presented by China's rise.

China's economic and military modernization represents a profound shift in the global balance of power. Fueled by decades of sustained economic growth, China has transformed from an agrarian society into a global economic and technological powerhouse. This economic ascendancy has provided the foundation for a significant military modernization drive, equipping the People's Liberation Army (PLA) with advanced weaponry and enhancing its operational capabilities.

China's military modernization extends beyond simply increasing its defense budget. It involves a comprehensive strategy aimed at achieving "military-civil fusion," a concept that integrates civilian and military research and development to accelerate technological advancements. This strategy leverages China's strengths in areas like artificial intelligence, big data, and advanced manufacturing to rapidly develop cutting-edge military technologies. This has yielded significant results, with China making rapid strides in areas such as hypersonic weapons, cyber warfare, artificial intelligence applications in warfare, and space-based capabilities, including anti-satellite technologies. The PLA Navy has expanded its fleet with aircraft carriers, destroyers, and submarines, projecting Chinese power beyond its immediate region through naval deployments and exercises in the South China Sea and beyond.

These developments reflect China's growing ambitions for regional hegemony and global influence. China seeks to assert its dominance in the Asia-Pacific region, challenging the existing US-led security architecture. Its assertive claims in the South China Sea, coupled with its military buildup, including the deployment of advanced missile systems on disputed islands, have raised serious concerns among regional neighbors like Japan, India, and the Philippines, and sparked increased tensions with the United States.

Furthermore, China aims to become a leading global power, exerting greater influence in international institutions and on the global stage. Its Belt and Road Initiative (BRI), a massive infrastructure development project spanning continents, is not merely an economic endeavor but also a geopolitical tool. The BRI aims to expand China's economic and political influence across Asia, Africa, and Europe, creating new trade routes, deepening economic interdependence, and enhancing China's strategic leverage.

China's economic and military modernization presents both opportunities and challenges for the international community.

While economic cooperation with China has benefited many countries through trade and investment, concerns remain about the potential for economic coercion, intellectual property theft, and unfair trade practices. The rise of Chinese military power has also led to increased geopolitical competition, raising concerns about potential conflict, the stability of the regional and global order, and the potential for an arms race in the Asia-Pacific region.

Navigating this complex landscape requires a multifaceted approach. This includes strengthening alliances and partnerships, investing in critical technologies, and developing clear and consistent strategies to address the challenges posed by China's rise. It also necessitates open and constructive dialogue with China to address areas of mutual concern and build a more stable and predictable relationship.

China's assertive actions in the South China Sea have significantly increased tensions in the region, altering the strategic landscape and raising concerns about regional stability and the potential for conflict. China claims almost the entirety of the South China Sea, overlapping with the claims of several other countries, including the Philippines, Vietnam, and Malaysia.

To solidify these claims, China has undertaken extensive island-building activities, creating artificial islands and constructing military installations on disputed reefs and shoals. These installations include airstrips, radar facilities, and missile defense systems, significantly enhancing China's military capabilities in the region and enabling it to project power more effectively.

Furthermore, China has engaged in a pattern of assertive behavior towards other claimants, including the harassment and intimidation of fishing vessels and coast guard ships from other countries operating within their exclusive economic zones. Chinese maritime law enforcement vessels frequently engage in dangerous maneuvers, such as close-range shadowing and water cannoning, aimed at asserting China's dominance and deterring other claimants from exercising their rights.

China also conducts regular military exercises in the South China Sea, including live-fire drills and deployments of warships and aircraft, demonstrating its military might and asserting its control over the area. These exercises often take place near disputed features and within the exclusive economic zones of other claimant states, raising concerns about the potential for miscalculation and accidental clashes.

China utilizes a large fleet of fishing vessels, often referred to as a "maritime militia," to assert its claims, intimidate other claimants, and disrupt fishing activities. These vessels often operate in concert with Chinese coast guard and naval vessels, creating a complex and potentially dangerous maritime environment.

Beyond the South China Sea, China's growing influence in the Philippines is another area of concern. While China has cultivated economic ties with the Philippines through investments in infrastructure projects under its Belt and Road

Initiative, these investments have also raised concerns about potential debt traps and undue Chinese influence over Philippine domestic policy.

Finally, China's pressure on Taiwan is a major source of regional and global tension. China views Taiwan as an integral part of its territory and has repeatedly asserted its right to reunify with the island, by force if necessary. In recent years, China has increased military pressure on Taiwan, including conducting frequent military exercises near the island and deploying military aircraft and naval vessels across the Taiwan Strait. These actions have significantly increased the risk of miscalculation and the potential for military conflict, raising serious concerns about regional and global stability.

China's assertive actions in the South China Sea, its growing influence in the Philippines, and its pressure on Taiwan have fundamentally altered the regional security landscape. These actions have raised concerns about freedom of navigation, the peaceful resolution of disputes, and the potential for escalation of tensions in the region.

China has made significant strides in key technological areas, including Artificial Intelligence (AI), 5G, and biotechnology, with profound implications for its global influence. China has emerged as a major player in AI, investing heavily in research and development and amassing vast troves of data. Chinese companies are at the forefront of AI development in areas such as facial recognition, natural language processing, and autonomous driving. This technological prowess has significant implications for national security, economic competitiveness, and even social control.

China was a pioneer in 5G deployment, boasting a vast and rapidly expanding 5G network. This advanced infrastructure provides a crucial foundation for the development of other emerging technologies, such as the Internet of Things (IoT), smart cities, and autonomous vehicles, giving China a significant edge in these rapidly evolving sectors.

In biotechnology, China is rapidly closing the gap with Western countries, making significant progress in areas such as gene editing, drug discovery, and personalized medicine. Chinese researchers are at the forefront of cutting-edge research in areas like CRISPR-Cas9 gene editing, with the potential for revolutionary breakthroughs in medicine and agriculture.

These technological advancements have significant implications for China's global dominance. Technological innovation is a key driver of economic growth, and China's advancements in AI, 5G, and biotechnology have the potential to fuel economic growth, enhance industrial competitiveness, and create new industries and jobs. Furthermore, these technologies have significant military applications, such as autonomous weapons systems, cyber warfare capabilities, and advanced surveillance technologies. This technological edge can enhance China's military capabilities and strengthen its position in the global power balance.

Beyond economic and military dominance, China's technological leadership can enhance its global influence. By setting international standards for emerging technologies and controlling critical technologies, China can exert significant influence over global technology ecosystems and shape the future of the digital world.

However, China's technological advancements also present challenges. Concerns have been raised about the potential for misuse of these technologies, such as the development of autonomous weapons systems that could raise ethical concerns and the potential for mass surveillance that could erode individual privacy. Intellectual property theft and concerns about data security are also significant issues, particularly given the potential for sensitive data to be exploited for strategic advantage.

In conclusion, China's rapid technological advancements in AI, 5G, and biotechnology have significant implications for its global dominance. While these advancements offer significant economic and strategic benefits, they also present challenges and require careful consideration of the ethical, social, and security implications. Navigating this complex landscape will require international cooperation, robust safeguards, and a commitment to responsible innovation.

The US response to China's rise is multifaceted, encompassing a range of strategies across various fronts. Economically, the US has implemented tariffs on Chinese goods to address trade imbalances and protect American industries, aiming to level the playing field and support domestic manufacturing. Efforts are underway to diversify supply chains, reducing reliance on Chinese manufacturing and mitigating potential disruptions. The US government is also investing heavily in domestic research and development, particularly in critical technologies like semiconductors, artificial intelligence, and quantum computing, to maintain its technological edge and ensure long-term economic competitiveness.

Geopolitically, the US is seeking to strengthen alliances and partnerships with like-minded countries to counter China's growing influence. This includes strengthening existing alliances with traditional partners like Japan, South Korea, and Australia, while also forging new partnerships with countries in the Indo-Pacific region, such as India and Vietnam. The US is also actively engaging in diplomatic efforts to counter China's Belt and Road Initiative, offering alternative infrastructure development models that prioritize transparency, sustainability, and debt sustainability.

The US is maintaining a strong military presence in the Indo-Pacific region, conducting regular military exercises and reinforcing alliances with regional partners to deter potential aggression and maintain freedom of navigation. The US is also modernizing its military capabilities, focusing on areas such as hypersonic weapons, artificial intelligence, and space-based capabilities to counter China's growing military power and ensure its ability to maintain a credible deterrent.

Technologically, the US government is implementing policies to protect critical technologies and prevent the transfer of sensitive technology to China. This includes restrictions on the sale of advanced technology to China, increased scrutiny of Chinese investments in US technology companies, and efforts to bolster domestic semiconductor manufacturing to reduce reliance on Chinese supply chains.

Diplomatically, the US is engaging with China on issues of mutual concern, such as climate change and global health, while also firmly addressing areas of disagreement, such as human rights, trade practices, and regional security. This approach aims to manage competition while seeking areas of cooperation where possible.

The US response to China's rise is a complex and ongoing process that requires a multifaceted approach. It involves a combination of economic, diplomatic, military, and technological measures aimed at maintaining US leadership, promoting a free and open Indo-Pacific region, and addressing the challenges posed by China's rise. This approach necessitates a long-term perspective, strategic agility, and close coordination with allies and partners to effectively navigate this complex and evolving relationship.

The US-China competition is a multifaceted phenomenon that extends far beyond traditional military and economic spheres, encompassing a complex web of interconnected challenges.

Economically, the competition centers around trade, investment, and technological dominance. The US seeks to address trade imbalances, protect intellectual property, and ensure fair market access for American businesses, while China aims to become the world's leading economic power, challenging US dominance in areas like manufacturing, technology, and finance. This economic rivalry manifests in various forms, including trade disputes, investment restrictions, and efforts to control critical supply chains, such as semiconductors and rare earth minerals.

The technological dimension of this competition is equally crucial. Both countries are investing heavily in research and development in critical technologies like artificial intelligence, 5G, biotechnology, and quantum computing. This fierce competition for technological supremacy has significant implications for national security, economic competitiveness, and global influence.

Military competition is another significant aspect of this rivalry. The US seeks to maintain military superiority in the Indo-Pacific region, while China is rapidly modernizing its military, expanding its naval capabilities, and developing advanced weapons systems, including hypersonic missiles and nuclear weapons. This military competition plays out in various arenas, including the South China Sea, where territorial disputes and military posturing are escalating tensions.

Diplomatically, the US is seeking to strengthen alliances and partnerships with like-minded countries to counter China's growing influence. This includes strengthening existing alliances with traditional partners like Japan, South Korea, and Australia, while also forging new partnerships with countries in the Indo-Pacific region, such as India and Vietnam. China, meanwhile, is actively expanding its diplomatic influence through initiatives like the Belt and Road Initiative, seeking to build relationships with countries across the globe and project its power on the world stage.

The competition extends beyond the economic and military spheres into the realm of ideology and values. The US champions democracy, human rights, and the rule of law, while China promotes its own model of authoritarian capitalism. This ideological competition plays out in various arenas, including international forums, media narratives, and the competition for influence in developing countries.

Furthermore, the competition extends to the realm of information and influence. Both countries engage in extensive propaganda and disinformation campaigns to shape global perceptions, influence public opinion, and undermine the credibility of their adversaries. This includes cyberattacks, the spread of misinformation, and efforts to manipulate public discourse through social media and other channels.

The US-China competition is a complex and multifaceted phenomenon with significant implications for the global order. It requires a comprehensive and nuanced approach that addresses the challenges and opportunities presented by this evolving rivalry. This includes strengthening alliances, investing in critical technologies, promoting democratic values, and developing effective strategies to counter disinformation and protect critical infrastructure.

# BEATING CHINA: A BLUEPRINT FOR AMERICAN VICTORY

"Victory" in the US-China rivalry is a complex and multifaceted concept that cannot be easily defined by a single metric or a single outcome. It is not about achieving complete dominance or the total defeat of one competitor but rather about ensuring the long-term security, prosperity, and global influence of the United States.

Maintaining US leadership in key technological areas is crucial. This involves ensuring continued American dominance in critical technologies like artificial intelligence, semiconductors, biotechnology, and quantum computing. This requires significant investments in research and development, fostering a vibrant innovation ecosystem that attracts and retains top talent in science and technology, and protecting intellectual property from theft and misuse by competitors.

Preserving US economic influence is another key component of "victory." This involves maintaining a strong and competitive economy, ensuring fair trade practices, and protecting American jobs. This may involve strengthening domestic manufacturing capabilities, diversifying supply chains to reduce reliance on China, and promoting sustainable economic growth that benefits all Americans.

Furthermore, maintaining US leadership in innovation is essential for long-term economic and strategic competitiveness. This requires fostering a culture of innovation, supporting entrepreneurship at all levels, and ensuring that the US remains at the forefront of technological advancement.

It's important to recognize that "victory" in this context is not about a zero-sum game. It likely involves a dynamic equilibrium where the US maintains a competitive advantage in key areas while also finding areas of cooperation with China on issues of mutual concern, such as climate change and global health. This requires a nuanced approach that balances competition with the need for cooperation to address global challenges.

Ultimately, "victory" in the US-China rivalry will be determined by the ability of the US to maintain its economic and technological leadership, uphold its democratic values, and effectively address the challenges of the 21st century while simultaneously managing the risks and complexities of this evolving relationship.

"Victory" in the US-China rivalry can be defined, in part, by the ability to preserve a free and open Indo-Pacific region, ensuring the security of key allies like the Philippines and Taiwan. This entails upholding the rules-based international order that has underpinned regional stability for decades.

Maintaining freedom of navigation and overflight in the South China Sea is paramount. China's assertive claims in the South China Sea, including its extensive island-building activities and the militarization of disputed features, challenge the freedom of navigation and overflight, a cornerstone of international law. The US must actively counter these claims, ensuring that all countries have unhindered access to the vital waterways of the region.

# BEATING CHINA: A BLUEPRINT FOR AMERICAN VICTORY

Deterrence of Chinese aggression against its neighbors is crucial. This requires a strong and credible US military presence in the region, including robust naval and air power. Strengthening alliances with regional partners like Japan, South Korea, Australia, and India is critical. These partnerships provide a framework for collective security, enabling the US and its allies to counter Chinese aggression more effectively. Providing these allies with the necessary military and diplomatic support, such as advanced military equipment, intelligence sharing, and joint military exercises, is essential to enhance their capabilities and deter potential aggression.

Ensuring the security of the Philippines and Taiwan is of paramount importance. The US has treaty obligations to defend the Philippines, and the security of Taiwan is a critical US national security interest. Maintaining the status quo across the Taiwan Strait and deterring any attempts by China to use force to reunify with the island are crucial to regional stability. This may involve providing Taiwan with the necessary defensive capabilities and clearly communicating the US commitment to Taiwan's security.

This definition of "victory" emphasizes the importance of maintaining a stable and secure regional order in the face of China's growing influence. It recognizes that the security of the US and its allies is inextricably linked to the security of the Indo-Pacific region. Upholding a rules-based international order, ensuring freedom of navigation, and deterring aggression are essential for long-term stability and prosperity in the region and beyond.

"Victory" in the US-China rivalry can be defined, in part, by the ability to uphold a rules-based international order and promote human rights and democratic values on the global stage. This goes beyond simply competing for economic or military dominance; it emphasizes the importance of upholding the principles that have underpinned global stability and prosperity for decades.

Actively defending and promoting the principles of international law, such as freedom of navigation, respect for territorial integrity, and the peaceful resolution of disputes, is crucial. This requires a concerted effort to counter China's attempts to unilaterally alter the status quo in the South China Sea and other regions while simultaneously working with allies and partners to uphold these principles in international forums.

Upholding human rights and democratic values is a core principle of US foreign policy. "Victory" in this context would involve effectively countering China's efforts to suppress human rights within its own borders, such as the documented human rights abuses against Uyghurs in Xinjiang and the suppression of dissent in Hong Kong. This could involve targeted sanctions, public diplomacy campaigns, and supporting international efforts to hold China accountable for its human rights record.

Furthermore, "victory" would involve advocating for human rights and democratic values in international forums like the United Nations and supporting human rights defenders around the world. This includes providing support to civil society organizations, promoting freedom of expression and assembly, and advocating for the rule of law globally.

This definition of "victory" emphasizes the importance of upholding US values and promoting a global order based on democracy, human rights, and the rule of law. It recognizes that the US has a moral and strategic interest in promoting these values globally. A world dominated by authoritarianism, where human rights are suppressed and international law is disregarded, would pose a significant threat to US interests and the stability of the international system.

"Victory" in the US-China rivalry can be defined, in part, by effectively preventing China from achieving its strategic objectives that undermine US interests. This requires a proactive and multifaceted approach that addresses the full spectrum of China's challenges to US leadership.

Preventing China from achieving military dominance in the Indo-Pacific region is paramount. This involves maintaining a strong military presence, including a robust naval and air power projection capability, in the region. Strengthening alliances with regional partners like Japan, South Korea, Australia, and India is crucial, enabling a collective response to potential Chinese aggression. Deterrence remains a key element, clearly communicating the consequences of any military action by China against its neighbors, such as an attack on Taiwan.

Countering China's efforts to dominate critical technologies is equally vital. This involves investing heavily in research and development in areas like artificial intelligence, semiconductors, biotechnology, and quantum computing, ensuring US technological leadership in these crucial fields. Protecting intellectual property from theft and misuse by Chinese entities is essential, as is mitigating the risks of technology transfer and ensuring the security of critical technology supply chains.

Preventing China from undermining the rules-based international order is another key aspect of "victory." This involves upholding international law, promoting freedom of navigation and overflight, and countering Chinese efforts to erode democratic values and human rights. This may involve diplomatic efforts to isolate China in international forums, supporting international institutions that uphold the rules-based order, and promoting alternative models of governance and development.

Countering China's attempts to expand its economic and political influence is also crucial. This involves diversifying supply chains to reduce reliance on China, mitigating the risks of economic dependence, and countering China's Belt and Road Initiative with alternative development models that prioritize transparency, sustainability, and respect for sovereignty.

By effectively preventing China from achieving its strategic objectives, the US can maintain its position as a leading global power, protect its national security interests, and promote a stable and prosperous international order. This requires a sustained and coordinated effort across all dimensions of the

US-China competition, including military, economic, diplomatic, technological, and informational.

Thesis Statement: The United States can and must prevail in its strategic competition with China through a comprehensive and sustained effort that leverages its strengths, mitigates its weaknesses, and prioritizes the defense of its vital interests. This effort must strategically integrate the contributions of innovative figures like Elon Musk, harnessing their capabilities while mitigating potential risks and ensuring alignment with broader national security and foreign policy objectives.

Part 1 – Understanding the Chinese Challenge

This report examines the multifaceted challenges posed by the rise of China. Understanding the Chinese Communist Party's (CCP) strategic blueprint is crucial to comprehending the nature and scope of these challenges. This first part of the report delves into the core tenets of the CCP's vision for China's future, exploring its ambitions for economic and military dominance, its efforts to reshape the global order, and its internal and external challenges.

Chapter 1, "The Chinese Communist Party's (CCP) Strategic Blueprint," serves as the foundation for this analysis. It will delve into the CCP's core ideology, its strategic objectives, and the key policies and initiatives driving its rise. By understanding the CCP's worldview and its long-term aspirations, we can better comprehend the nature of the challenges it poses and develop effective strategies to address them.

Chapter 1 – The Chinese Communist Party's (CCP) Strategic Blueprint

This chapter delves into the core tenets of the CCP's long-term strategic objectives, examining its ambitions for global influence, ideological dominance, and ultimately, the displacement of the US as the dominant global power. The CCP's strategic blueprint outlines a vision for China that extends far beyond mere economic growth and military modernization. It encompasses a broader ambition to reshape the international order, establishing China as a global leader not only in economic terms, but also in political, military, and ideological spheres.

A key objective is to significantly enhance China's global influence. This involves expanding its economic and political reach through initiatives like the Belt and Road Initiative, a massive infrastructure development project that aims to connect China with countries across Asia, Africa, and Europe. By investing in key infrastructure projects, such as ports, railways, and energy pipelines, China seeks to deepen its economic ties with partner countries, expand its markets, and secure access to critical resources.

Furthermore, China aims to increase its political influence by cultivating relationships with countries across the globe, leveraging its economic power to build alliances and partnerships. This includes expanding its diplomatic presence, engaging in active public diplomacy campaigns, and increasing its representation in international institutions such as the United Nations and the World Bank.

Another critical objective is to promote its own political and ideological model. The CCP seeks to project its unique brand of "socialism with Chinese characteristics," emphasizing the superiority of its one-party rule and its economic development model as an alternative to Western democracy. This involves showcasing China's economic achievements as evidence of the superiority of its system and actively promoting its model to other developing countries.

Ultimately, the CCP aims to diminish US global influence and eventually displace the US as the dominant global power. This involves challenging US leadership in key areas such as technology, trade, and military power. China seeks to become a leading technological power, competing with the US in areas like artificial intelligence, 5G, and biotechnology. Economically, China aims to surpass the US as the world's largest economy, while simultaneously challenging US economic dominance through trade practices, investment strategies, and the development of alternative international economic institutions.

This chapter will explore these long-term strategic objectives in greater detail, examining the key policies and initiatives that the CCP is pursuing to achieve them, such as the "Made in China 2025" initiative, the military modernization of the People's Liberation Army, and the expansion of its global media influence. By analyzing these objectives and the means by which the CCP seeks to achieve them, we can gain a deeper understanding of the challenges posed by China's rise and develop effective strategies to address them.

The CCP employs a multifaceted approach to advance its strategic objectives, utilizing a combination of economic, military, diplomatic, and informational tools. The Belt and Road Initiative (BRI) serves as a cornerstone of this strategy. While ostensibly focused on economic development, the BRI is more than just an infrastructure project. It functions as a tool for expanding China's global influence, deepening its economic and political ties with partner countries, and projecting its power across the globe. Through investments in ports, railways, and other critical infrastructure, China seeks to enhance its connectivity, expand its markets, and secure access to vital resources.

Economic coercion is another key tactic employed by the CCP. China leverages its economic power to exert pressure on other countries, utilizing trade restrictions, investment restrictions, and the use of "debt-trap diplomacy." This strategy involves extending loans for infrastructure projects through the BRI, often with unsustainable terms, leaving recipient countries heavily indebted to China and potentially compromising their sovereignty.

Military expansionism is a critical component of China's strategy to assert its regional and global influence. The People's Liberation Army (PLA) has undergone significant modernization, with investments in advanced weaponry, including aircraft carriers, stealth fighters, and long-range missiles. The PLA has expanded its military presence in the South China Sea, building artificial islands and deploying military assets in the region, challenging freedom of navigation, and increasing regional tensions.

Influence operations are another crucial element of China's strategy. The CCP employs a range of tactics to shape global perceptions and influence public opinion, including propaganda campaigns, disinformation operations, and the use of state-sponsored media outlets like CGTN and Xinhua News Agency. These efforts aim to undermine the credibility of Western democracies, promote the CCP's own narrative, and cultivate a favorable international image.

Finally, technological dominance is a key objective. China is investing heavily in critical technologies such as artificial intelligence, 5G, and biotechnology, aiming to surpass the US in these areas. This technological advancement has significant implications for military power, economic competitiveness, and global influence.

These tactics, employed in concert, reflect the CCP's multifaceted approach to achieving its strategic objectives. Understanding these tactics is crucial for developing effective strategies to counter China's rise and protect US interests in a competitive and increasingly complex global environment.

Examining specific case studies provides crucial insights into the CCP's tactics. In the South China Sea, China has undertaken extensive island-building activities, creating artificial islands and militarizing them with airstrips, radar facilities, and missile systems. These actions directly challenge freedom of navigation and overflight, a cornerstone of the international rules-based order. China's assertive maritime claims, backed by a growing naval presence and the use of its maritime militia to intimidate other claimants, have significantly increased tensions in the region. These actions not only assert China's territorial claims but also aim to establish its military dominance and deter other countries from operating freely in these vital waterways.

In the Philippines, the CCP has employed a combination of economic inducements and coercive tactics to expand its influence. The Belt and Road Initiative has seen significant Chinese investment in infrastructure projects in the Philippines, raising concerns about potential debt traps and undue Chinese influence over Philippine domestic policy. These investments can create economic dependence and potentially limit the Philippines' policy autonomy. Simultaneously, China has engaged in activities that undermine Philippine sovereignty, such as harassing Filipino fishermen in their traditional fishing grounds, encroaching on Philippine territory in the South China Sea, and employing coercive tactics to pressure the Philippines to acquiesce to China's demands.

China's pressure on Taiwan is a critical aspect of its broader strategic objectives. The CCP views Taiwan as an integral part of China and has repeatedly asserted its right to reunify with the island, by force if necessary. This pressure manifests in various forms, including military intimidation through frequent military exercises near Taiwan, diplomatic isolation of Taiwan by limiting its international space, and economic coercion to limit Taiwan's international engagement. These actions aim to weaken Taiwan's international support, erode its confidence, and ultimately compel its eventual reunification with China.

These case studies demonstrate the multifaceted nature of the CCP's tactics. They employ a combination of economic, military, diplomatic, and informational tools to advance their strategic interests, challenge the existing international order, and expand their global influence. Understanding these specific examples is crucial for developing effective strategies to counter China's rise and safeguard US interests and the rules-based international order. This includes strengthening alliances with regional partners, bolstering the defense capabilities of key allies like the Philippines and Taiwan, and developing robust countermeasures to address Chinese coercion and influence operations.

The CCP likely views Elon Musk and his companies, particularly Tesla and SpaceX, as a complex and multifaceted phenomenon with both potential opportunities and significant challenges.

On one hand, Musk's companies present potential opportunities for China. Tesla's significant presence in China, including its manufacturing plant in Shanghai, provides China with access to cutting-edge electric vehicle technology, including advancements in battery technology, autonomous driving software, and vehicle design. This can contribute to China's ambitions to become a global leader in the electric vehicle market and enhance its domestic automotive industry. SpaceX's advancements in space technology, such as reusable rockets and satellite internet services, could also offer potential areas for collaboration, potentially benefiting China's own space exploration programs and providing access to advanced space technologies.

However, Musk and his companies also present significant challenges to the CCP. Tesla, despite its operations in China, represents a successful example of American technological innovation and entrepreneurialism. Tesla's success, particularly in areas like autonomous driving and battery technology, can challenge China's ambitions to dominate the global electric vehicle market and maintain its technological edge. SpaceX, with its advanced launch capabilities and ambitions for space exploration, including missions to Mars, could enhance US military and strategic advantages in space, potentially countering China's growing space ambitions.

Furthermore, Musk's public pronouncements and actions, particularly his criticism of the Chinese government on issues like free speech and human rights, can be seen as a challenge to the CCP's narrative and its efforts to project a positive image internationally. Musk's outspoken views can undermine the CCP's efforts to portray China as a responsible global leader and can resonate with audiences who are critical of China's human rights record.

To address these challenges and potentially leverage the opportunities presented by Musk's companies, the CCP may employ a range of strategies. These may include efforts to co-opt Musk and his companies, encouraging collaboration and investment in China while subtly exerting influence over their operations. The CCP may also intensify its efforts to develop and promote its own domestic competitors in the electric vehicle and space industries, seeking to challenge Tesla and SpaceX directly.

Furthermore, the CCP may seek to control Musk's companies operating within China through regulations, data security requirements, and other measures. Finally, the CCP may utilize state-controlled media and social media influencers to counter Musk's public statements, project a more favorable image of China, and shape public perception of his companies and their activities.

The CCP's perception of Musk and his companies is likely to evolve as the geopolitical landscape shifts, as these companies continue to grow and innovate, and as the US-China competition intensifies. The CCP will need to carefully assess the potential opportunities and challenges presented by Musk's companies and develop strategies to mitigate the risks and leverage any potential benefits.

Chapter 2 – China's Economic and Technological Powerhouse

China has made significant strides in its economic and technological advancement, driven by ambitious government initiatives and a focus on key sectors. "Made in China 2025," a strategic plan aimed at upgrading China's manufacturing base, outlines ambitious goals for achieving global leadership in ten key industries, including information technology, robotics, and advanced materials. This initiative leverages government subsidies, state-owned enterprises, and targeted investments to foster innovation and develop domestic champions in these sectors.

China is also investing heavily in emerging technologies, such as artificial intelligence (AI), 5G, and quantum computing.

These technologies are seen as crucial for future economic growth, military dominance, and global influence. The Chinese government has made significant investments in AI research and development, established national laboratories focused on AI, and encouraged the development of AI applications in various sectors, from surveillance and security to healthcare and finance. China has also been a leader in the deployment of 5G technology, building a vast and rapidly expanding 5G network that will underpin future technological advancements, such as the Internet of Things (IoT) and autonomous vehicles. This technological infrastructure provides a crucial foundation for China's future economic and technological development.

However, China's economic and technological advancements have also raised concerns. One major concern is intellectual property theft. China has been accused of systematically stealing intellectual property from foreign companies through various means, including cyber espionage, forced technology transfer, and the exploitation of foreign companies operating in China. This includes the theft of trade secrets, the misappropriation of copyrighted materials, and the forced transfer of technology in exchange for market access. This has significant implications for global innovation and competitiveness, as it undermines the incentives for research and development in other countries and creates an unfair playing field for foreign companies.

Furthermore, China's economic and technological ambitions are often pursued through state-led initiatives and government intervention, raising concerns about fair competition and market distortions. The Chinese government's support for domestic companies, including through subsidies and preferential treatment, can create an uneven playing field for foreign competitors. This can lead to concerns about unfair trade practices and the potential for market dominance by Chinese state-owned enterprises.

In conclusion, China's economic and technological advancements are significant and have profound implications for the global balance of power. While these advancements have contributed to China's economic growth and development, concerns remain regarding intellectual property theft, unfair competition, and the potential for these advancements to be used for military and strategic advantage. Addressing these concerns requires a multifaceted approach, including strengthening international cooperation on intellectual property protection, promoting fair trade practices, and ensuring a level playing field for global competition.

The rise of China presents a significant challenge to US economic dominance, posing threats such as supply chain disruptions, the erosion of US technological leadership, and the potential for economic coercion.

The COVID-19 pandemic starkly highlighted the vulnerabilities of global supply chains heavily reliant on China. Disruptions to Chinese manufacturing, such as factory closures due to lockdowns, transportation bottlenecks, and port congestion, can have cascading effects on global supply chains, impacting industries across the US economy. This includes critical sectors such as electronics, automotive, and pharmaceuticals, leading to shortages, production delays, and inflationary pressures. The reliance on China for key components and intermediate goods leaves the US economy vulnerable to potential disruptions caused by geopolitical events, natural disasters, or deliberate Chinese actions.

Erosion of US technological leadership is another key concern. China is investing heavily in critical technologies like artificial intelligence, 5G, semiconductors, and biotechnology, aiming to surpass the US in these areas. This competition poses a significant challenge to US technological dominance, potentially impacting US economic competitiveness, national security, and global influence. China's aggressive pursuit of technological advancement, coupled with its use of industrial policies, such as government subsidies and intellectual property theft, creates an uneven playing field for US companies and threatens to erode US technological advantages.

Economic coercion is another potential threat. China's growing economic power allows it to exert pressure on other countries through trade restrictions, investment restrictions, and the use of "debt-trap diplomacy." This can limit the economic freedom of other countries, undermine their ability to compete in the global market, and potentially coerce them into making policy decisions that align with China's interests. For example, China can use its economic leverage to pressure countries to refrain from criticizing China's human rights record, to limit their engagement with Taiwan, or to adopt policies that favor Chinese companies.

Addressing these challenges requires a multifaceted approach. This includes diversifying supply chains to reduce reliance on China, investing in domestic manufacturing and research and development to bolster US competitiveness in key industries, strengthening alliances with like-minded countries to counter Chinese economic influence, and developing strategies to counter Chinese economic coercion. This may involve strengthening international trade rules, promoting fair competition, and ensuring that US companies have access to fair and open markets.

The competitive landscape between Chinese and US companies is rapidly evolving, particularly in the electric vehicle (EV) sector. Tesla, a leading US EV manufacturer, faces stiff competition from a growing number of Chinese companies, including BYD, NIO, Xpeng, and Li Auto.

These Chinese companies are rapidly gaining ground in the global EV market. BYD, a leading Chinese EV manufacturer with a diverse product portfolio, including passenger cars, buses, and trucks, has a strong presence in the Chinese market and is rapidly expanding its global reach through strategic partnerships and investments. NIO, known for its high-end electric vehicles and advanced battery technology, has established a strong brand in the Chinese market and is expanding its global footprint with plans to enter new markets in Europe and North America. Xpeng, a more technology-focused company, offers advanced driver-assistance systems and innovative features, challenging Tesla in the area of vehicle software and autonomous driving. Li Auto specializes in extended-range electric vehicles, combining electric motors with a gasoline engine for extended range, appealing to consumers with range anxiety.

The competition between these companies centers around key technologies like battery technology, autonomous driving, and vehicle software. Chinese companies are making significant strides in these areas, challenging Tesla's technological leadership. Chinese companies often benefit from government support, access to a large domestic market, and a well-developed supply chain for EV components, giving them a significant cost advantage.

Tesla faces several challenges in this competitive landscape. The intense competition from Chinese EV manufacturers, with their aggressive expansion strategies and government support, poses a significant threat to Tesla's market share. Concerns about data security also arise from Tesla's operations in China, with potential risks of data access and control by the Chinese government. Furthermore, the escalating US-China rivalry poses geopolitical risks for Tesla's operations in China, including potential trade restrictions, regulatory hurdles, and increased scrutiny from the Chinese government.

The competitive landscape between Tesla and Chinese EV manufacturers is dynamic and evolving rapidly. While Tesla maintains a strong brand and technological advantage in certain areas, it faces significant challenges from a growing number of Chinese competitors. The outcome of this competition will have significant implications for the global EV market, the future of the automotive industry, and the broader US-China technological rivalry.

## Chapter 3 – Assessing China's Vulnerabilities

The Chinese economic and political system, while demonstrating remarkable growth and stability, faces several significant vulnerabilities that could pose challenges to its long-term trajectory.

Economically, China faces a slowdown in growth momentum. Declining productivity growth, an aging population, and increasing debt levels are creating headwinds for the Chinese economy. The "zero-COVID" policy, while crucial in the early stages of the pandemic, has also significantly impacted economic activity, disrupting supply chains, dampening consumer confidence, and hindering economic growth. Maintaining sustained economic growth and addressing the challenges of an aging population, such as providing adequate healthcare and social security for the elderly, will be crucial for China's continued development and social stability.

Social unrest is another significant challenge. Despite significant economic progress, China faces growing social inequality and regional disparities. Rapid urbanization has led to social unrest and environmental degradation, particularly in coastal areas. Rising unemployment, particularly among young people, and concerns about income inequality and social justice can pose significant challenges to social stability. The CCP faces the challenge of addressing these concerns while maintaining social control and ensuring political stability.

Environmental challenges are also a major concern. China faces severe environmental issues, including air and water pollution, deforestation, and the impact of climate change. These environmental challenges pose significant threats to public health, agricultural productivity, and economic development. Addressing these challenges requires significant investment in environmental protection, a shift towards a more sustainable development model, and a willingness to prioritize environmental concerns alongside economic growth.

Furthermore, the CCP's authoritarian model, while contributing to rapid economic growth, also presents limitations. The lack of political pluralism, suppression of dissent, and limited freedom of expression can stifle innovation, hinder the development of a truly vibrant civil society, and create an environment where critical thinking and independent decision-making are discouraged. This lack of flexibility and adaptability may prove to be a significant obstacle in addressing complex challenges of the 21st century, such as technological disruption, climate change, and the need for rapid societal and economic transformation.

These vulnerabilities, if not effectively addressed, could pose significant challenges to China's long-term stability and prosperity. The CCP will need to navigate these challenges effectively while maintaining its political legitimacy and ensuring continued economic growth and social stability.

The potential for internal instability within China poses significant risks to its regional and global ambitions. While China has experienced remarkable economic growth and political stability in recent decades, several internal factors could potentially destabilize the country and hinder its rise as a global power.

Growing income inequality is a significant concern. The gap between the rich and the poor continues to widen, with a small segment of the population accumulating a disproportionate share of wealth. This inequality can fuel social unrest and discontent, particularly among younger generations who face challenges such as rising housing costs and limited job opportunities.

Regional disparities also contribute to social and economic instability. While coastal regions have experienced rapid economic growth, many inland regions continue to lag behind, facing higher levels of poverty and unemployment. This uneven development can lead to resentment and social unrest among those left behind by economic progress.

Environmental degradation is another critical challenge. China faces severe environmental issues, including air and water pollution, deforestation, and the impact of climate change. These environmental challenges can have significant social and economic consequences, leading to public health crises, agricultural disruptions, and displacement of populations. Severe environmental degradation can also trigger social unrest and undermine public confidence in the government's ability to address critical issues.

China's rapidly aging population presents significant demographic challenges. A declining birth rate and an increasing elderly population will strain the social safety net, increase healthcare costs, and potentially slow economic growth. This demographic shift could also impact the country's long-term competitiveness and military strength.

The CCP's authoritarian model, while contributing to economic growth, also presents limitations. The lack of political pluralism, suppression of dissent, and limited freedom of expression can stifle innovation, hinder the development of a truly vibrant civil society, and create an environment where critical thinking and independent decision-making are discouraged. This lack of flexibility and adaptability may prove to be a significant obstacle in addressing complex challenges and maintaining long-term stability.

If internal instability were to escalate, it could have significant repercussions for China's regional and global ambitions. Internal unrest, social upheaval, and economic slowdown could divert resources from military modernization, foreign policy initiatives, and economic development, hindering China's ability to compete with the US on the global stage. It could also undermine China's image as a stable and rising power, eroding international confidence in its long-term stability and economic prospects.

The potential impact of Elon Musk's companies, particularly Tesla and SpaceX, on the Chinese economy and society is multifaceted and presents both opportunities and significant challenges for the Chinese government.

Tesla's presence in China has already had a significant impact. Tesla's Gigafactory Shanghai has become a major player in

China's electric vehicle market, contributing to domestic production and technological advancements. Tesla's success in the Chinese market has spurred competition among domestic EV manufacturers, driving innovation and technological development in areas such as battery technology, autonomous driving, and vehicle software. However, Tesla's success also poses challenges. Tesla's technological advancements and its ability to capture market share can threaten the ambitions of Chinese EV companies to dominate the global market. Moreover, Tesla's operations in China raise concerns about data security and the potential for sensitive data to be accessed or controlled by the Chinese government.

SpaceX also presents both opportunities and challenges for China. SpaceX's advancements in space technology, such as reusable rockets and satellite internet services, could offer potential areas for collaboration, such as joint space exploration projects or the development of satellite communication infrastructure. However, SpaceX's technological prowess, particularly in areas like satellite internet and space launch capabilities, could enhance US military and strategic advantages in space, potentially countering China's growing space ambitions.

Furthermore, Musk's public pronouncements and actions, particularly his criticism of the Chinese government on issues like free speech and human rights, can be seen as a challenge to the CCP's narrative and its efforts to project a positive image internationally. These statements can undermine the CCP's efforts to portray China as a responsible global leader and can resonate with audiences who are critical of China's human rights record.

The Chinese government is likely to respond to these challenges and opportunities in various ways. It may seek to co-opt Tesla and SpaceX by encouraging collaboration and investment in China while simultaneously exerting influence over their operations and data access. The Chinese government may also intensify its support for domestic competitors in the EV and space sectors, providing subsidies, preferential treatment, and other forms of support to enable them to compete more effectively with Tesla and SpaceX.

Furthermore, the Chinese government may seek to control Tesla's operations within China through regulations, data security requirements, and other measures to mitigate potential risks and ensure that Tesla's activities align with China's national interests. The Chinese government may also utilize state-controlled media and social media influencers to counter Musk's public statements, project a more favorable image of China, and promote the achievements of Chinese companies in the EV and space sectors.

The Chinese government's response to Elon Musk and his companies will likely evolve as the geopolitical landscape shifts and as these companies continue to grow and innovate. The Chinese government will need to carefully assess the potential opportunities and challenges presented by these companies and develop strategies to mitigate the risks and leverage any potential benefits for China's own economic and strategic interests.

# BEATING CHINA: A BLUEPRINT FOR AMERICAN VICTORY

Part 2 – America's Strengths and Strategies

This section, Part 2: America's Strengths and Strategies, explores the critical strengths and strategic approaches the United States can leverage to counter the challenges posed by China's rise. Chapter 4, "Unleashing American Innovation," delves into the crucial role of innovation in maintaining US economic and technological leadership. It will examine the policies and investments necessary to foster a vibrant innovation ecosystem, cultivate a skilled workforce, and protect American intellectual property. By harnessing the power of American ingenuity, the United States can maintain its competitive edge in key technologies and drive economic growth.

Chapter 4 – Unleashing American Innovation

Maintaining US leadership in key technologies like artificial intelligence (AI), biotechnology, quantum computing, and semiconductors is paramount for economic growth, national security, and global influence. These technologies are driving innovation across sectors, from healthcare and transportation to defense and national security. US leadership in these areas is essential to ensure economic competitiveness, maintain a strong national defense, and address critical global challenges such as climate change and pandemics.

To maintain this leadership, the United States must prioritize several key strategies. Increased public and private investment in fundamental and applied research is crucial to drive innovation in these fields. This includes supporting university research through robust funding mechanisms, investing in national laboratories that conduct cutting-edge research, and providing incentives for private sector investment in research and development.

Fostering a vibrant innovation ecosystem is essential for translating research breakthroughs into commercial products and services. This requires creating an environment that supports entrepreneurship, attracts and retains top talent from around the world, and encourages risk-taking. Policies that promote access to capital, facilitate the commercialization of research, and protect intellectual property are critical to fostering a thriving innovation ecosystem.

Addressing the skills gap is another crucial element. Investing in education and workforce development programs is essential to ensure a skilled workforce capable of driving innovation in these critical technologies. This includes strengthening STEM education at all levels, expanding access to higher education, and promoting lifelong learning opportunities to equip the workforce with the skills needed to thrive in a rapidly evolving technological landscape.

Finally, protecting critical technologies from foreign interference and ensuring the security of supply chains is essential. This may include restrictions on the export of sensitive technologies, increased scrutiny of foreign investment, and efforts to bolster domestic production of critical components such as semiconductors.

By prioritizing these strategies, the United States can maintain its technological leadership, ensure its economic competitiveness, and safeguard its national security in the face of growing global competition, particularly from China.

This chapter will delve deeper into these strategies, exploring specific policy recommendations and examining the challenges and opportunities associated with each.

Prioritizing investments in research and development (R&D) and strengthening domestic semiconductor manufacturing are crucial for maintaining US technological leadership and economic competitiveness in the face of growing global competition, particularly from China.

Investing heavily in R&D across a wide range of critical technologies is paramount. This includes artificial intelligence, biotechnology, quantum computing, advanced materials, and other emerging technologies that will shape the future. Increased public and private investment in fundamental and applied research is essential to drive innovation and maintain a competitive edge. This requires robust funding for university research, supporting the work of national laboratories, and providing significant tax incentives for private sector investment in R&D.

Strengthening domestic semiconductor manufacturing is equally critical. Semiconductors are the foundation of modern technology, powering everything from smartphones and computers to automobiles and advanced weaponry. A strong domestic semiconductor industry is crucial for national security, economic competitiveness, and technological innovation. The US must take steps to bolster domestic semiconductor production, including providing incentives for domestic manufacturing, investing in advanced semiconductor manufacturing facilities, and strengthening supply chain resilience to reduce reliance on foreign suppliers, particularly from China.

These investments will not only drive innovation and economic growth but also enhance US national security. Technological leadership in critical areas like AI and semiconductors is essential for maintaining a strong national defense, developing advanced military capabilities, and addressing emerging security challenges such as cyber threats and the development of autonomous weapons systems.

Furthermore, a strong domestic semiconductor industry is vital for ensuring the long-term competitiveness of US industries across various sectors, from automotive to aerospace and defense. By investing in R&D and strengthening domestic semiconductor manufacturing, the US can maintain its technological edge, safeguard its national security, and ensure its continued prosperity in the face of growing global competition.

Protecting intellectual property and countering Chinese espionage activities are crucial for maintaining US technological leadership and economic competitiveness. The theft of intellectual property by Chinese entities, including state-sponsored actors, has become a significant concern, undermining the incentives for innovation and eroding US technological advantages.

Cyber espionage poses a major threat. Chinese state-sponsored actors are increasingly sophisticated in their cyber capabilities, targeting US companies and government agencies to steal sensitive data, including trade secrets, research and development information, and military plans. These cyberattacks not only harm individual companies but also undermine US national security and economic competitiveness.

Forced technology transfer is another significant challenge. Chinese authorities often pressure foreign companies operating in China to transfer sensitive technology to Chinese partners as a condition for market access. This practice not only harms US companies but also undermines US technological leadership by allowing China to acquire critical technologies without investing in their own research and development.

The misappropriation of trade secrets, including through industrial espionage and the theft of intellectual property by Chinese students and researchers, is another serious concern. These activities undermine the hard-earned innovations of US companies and stifle American competitiveness.

To counter these threats, the US must strengthen its efforts to protect intellectual property. This includes enhancing cybersecurity measures to protect critical infrastructure and sensitive data from cyberattacks originating from China. This may involve investing in advanced cybersecurity technologies, improving cybersecurity training and awareness, and strengthening international cooperation to combat cyber threats.

Implementing stricter controls on the export of sensitive technologies to China is also crucial. This includes carefully reviewing export licenses, identifying and mitigating potential risks of technology transfer, and ensuring that sensitive technologies are not used to develop military capabilities that could be used against the US.

Increasing efforts to investigate and prosecute cases of intellectual property theft by Chinese entities, both in the US and internationally, is essential. This includes strengthening law enforcement cooperation with international partners, improving the ability to track and disrupt cyberattacks, and enhancing the legal framework to deter and punish intellectual property theft.

Finally, identifying and countering Chinese influence operations aimed at stealing intellectual property or compromising US research and development efforts is crucial. This may involve strengthening counterintelligence capabilities, raising public awareness of the threat of foreign interference, and promoting best practices for protecting sensitive information.

By taking these steps, the US can better protect its intellectual property, maintain its technological edge, and ensure that the benefits of innovation are shared by American businesses and workers while also countering the growing threat of Chinese espionage and ensuring US national security.

Elon Musk serves as a prominent example of the role of entrepreneurs in driving American innovation and technological advancement. His companies, Tesla and SpaceX, have revolutionized their respective industries, pushing the boundaries of technological innovation and inspiring a new generation of entrepreneurs and innovators.

Tesla has played a pivotal role in accelerating the transition to electric vehicles, challenging the dominance of traditional automotive manufacturers and demonstrating the viability and desirability of electric vehicles on a mass scale. Tesla's innovations in battery technology, autonomous driving, and vehicle design have not only transformed the automotive industry but also spurred competition and innovation among other automakers, both domestically and internationally. Tesla's success has demonstrated the potential for disruptive innovation and the importance of challenging established norms and pursuing ambitious technological goals.

SpaceX has revolutionized space transportation, significantly reducing the cost of access to space and opening up new possibilities for space exploration and commercial space activities. SpaceX's reusable rockets have dramatically lowered the cost of launching payloads into orbit, enabling more frequent and affordable space missions, including satellite launches for communication, Earth observation, and other applications. SpaceX's achievements have not only advanced space exploration but have also inspired a new era of commercial space activity, with numerous companies developing new technologies and services for the space economy.

Beyond their specific technological achievements, Musk's companies have also had a significant impact on the broader innovation ecosystem in the United States. They have inspired a new generation of entrepreneurs and innovators, demonstrating the potential for disruptive innovation and the importance of pursuing ambitious goals. Tesla and SpaceX have also attracted significant investment to the US technology sector, fostering a vibrant ecosystem of startups and supporting the development of new technologies in areas such as artificial intelligence, robotics, and advanced materials.

Furthermore, Musk's public pronouncements and advocacy for technological advancement have played a crucial role in shaping public discourse and inspiring a new generation of engineers and scientists. His vision for the future, including the colonization of Mars, has captured the imagination of people around the world and inspired a renewed sense of optimism about the potential of human ingenuity.

It is important to acknowledge that Musk's companies and his leadership style also present certain challenges and complexities. These include concerns about data privacy, workplace safety, and the potential impact of some of his technological ventures on society. However, despite these challenges, Elon Musk and his companies serve as powerful examples of the transformative power of American entrepreneurship and the importance of fostering an environment that supports innovation and risk-taking. By supporting and encouraging such entrepreneurial endeavors, the US can maintain its technological leadership and continue to drive innovation and economic growth in the 21st century.

Government policies aimed at supporting or regulating companies like SpaceX and Tesla present a complex set of potential benefits and risks. On one hand, government support can play a crucial role in driving innovation and fostering economic growth. Research grants, tax incentives, and regulatory frameworks can incentivize innovation and accelerate the development of cutting-edge technologies in sectors such as electric vehicles, space exploration, artificial intelligence, and renewable energy. This can foster a competitive advantage for US companies in these crucial sectors, leading to job creation, economic growth, and improved living standards. Furthermore, government policies can be used to address national security concerns, such as ensuring the security of critical technologies and supply chains and maintaining US technological leadership in areas like space exploration and defense.

However, government intervention also carries significant risks. Government subsidies and other forms of support can distort market competition, potentially creating an uneven playing field and hindering the development of innovative solutions from smaller companies or startups. Excessive regulation can stifle innovation by increasing costs, delaying product development, and hindering entrepreneurial activity. Over-reliance on government support can create an environment where companies become dependent on government subsidies and may be less incentivized to develop sustainable and independent business models.

Furthermore, government support for emerging technologies raises ethical considerations. The development and deployment of advanced technologies such as artificial intelligence and autonomous vehicles raise concerns about potential job displacement, the ethical implications of AI decision-making, and the environmental consequences of certain technologies.

Balancing these potential benefits and risks requires a nuanced approach. Government policies should be carefully designed to encourage innovation while minimizing market distortions and addressing potential ethical concerns. This may involve targeted support for specific areas of research and development, fostering healthy competition, and establishing clear ethical guidelines for the development and deployment of new technologies.

Chapter 5 – Building a Resilient Economy

Reducing dependence on China for critical goods and technologies is a key strategic priority for the United States to ensure its economic and national security in a rapidly changing geopolitical landscape. Over-reliance on China for essential goods and technologies creates vulnerabilities in the US supply chains, exposes the US economy to potential disruptions, and undermines US technological leadership.

Diversifying supply chains is crucial to mitigate these risks. This involves identifying and cultivating alternative sources of critical components and raw materials, such as semiconductors, rare earth minerals, and pharmaceuticals. This can be achieved through a combination of strategies, including reshoring, nearshoring, and friend-shoring. Reshoring involves bringing manufacturing back to the United States, creating domestic jobs, and strengthening domestic supply chains. Nearshoring involves relocating manufacturing to countries closer to the US, such as Mexico or Canada, reducing transportation times and improving supply chain agility. Friend-shoring prioritizes trade and investment with trusted allies and partners, such as countries in Europe and Asia, strengthening economic and security ties while reducing reliance on China.

Bolstering domestic manufacturing capabilities is essential for ensuring the long-term security and competitiveness of the US economy. This involves investing in advanced manufacturing technologies, such as robotics, automation, and artificial intelligence, to enhance productivity and competitiveness. Supporting domestic companies in key industries, such as semiconductors, pharmaceuticals, and advanced materials, through targeted incentives, tax breaks, and government procurement programs is crucial. This will encourage domestic production, create high-skilled jobs, and strengthen the US industrial base.

Investing in critical technologies is vital for maintaining US technological leadership and national security. This includes increasing investment in research and development in areas such as semiconductors, artificial intelligence, biotechnology, and quantum computing. Strengthening domestic production of critical components such as semiconductors is crucial to ensure a secure and reliable supply chain for these technologies. This will reduce reliance on foreign suppliers, particularly from China, and ensure the US has access to the critical technologies necessary for economic growth, national security, and global competitiveness.

By implementing these strategies, the US can reduce its reliance on China for critical goods and technologies, enhance its economic and national security, and maintain its global competitiveness in the face of growing geopolitical challenges. This will require a coordinated effort across government, industry, and academia to strengthen domestic capabilities, diversify supply chains, and foster a robust and resilient US economy.

Reshoring manufacturing and strengthening domestic supply chains, including those that rely on the Panama Canal, is a critical component of US economic and national security strategy. Over-reliance on global supply chains, particularly those heavily concentrated in China, has exposed the US economy to significant vulnerabilities. Disruptions to these supply chains, whether due to geopolitical events, natural disasters, or pandemics, can have severe consequences for the US economy, including shortages of essential goods, disruptions to critical industries, and inflationary pressures.

By reshoring manufacturing, the US can reduce its reliance on foreign suppliers and enhance its economic resilience. This involves incentivizing companies to relocate production facilities back to the US, providing tax breaks, and improving the business climate for domestic manufacturing. This can create high-quality jobs, boost domestic production, and strengthen the US manufacturing base, which has declined significantly in recent decades.

Strengthening domestic supply chains requires a multifaceted approach. This includes identifying critical supply chain vulnerabilities, diversifying sources of raw materials and components, and investing in domestic production of essential goods. This may involve supporting the development of domestic industries in key sectors, such as semiconductors, pharmaceuticals, and critical minerals, ensuring a reliable and secure supply of these essential goods.

The Panama Canal plays a crucial role in global trade, connecting the Atlantic and Pacific Oceans and facilitating the movement of goods between North and South America, Asia, and Europe. Strengthening domestic supply chains that rely on the Panama Canal is essential for maintaining US economic competitiveness and ensuring the flow of critical goods. This may involve investing in infrastructure improvements to enhance the efficiency of the Panama Canal, such as expanding capacity and improving navigation technology. It may also involve diversifying shipping routes, exploring alternative transportation options, and strengthening partnerships with countries in the region to ensure the smooth and uninterrupted flow of goods through the Panama Canal.

By reshoring manufacturing, strengthening domestic supply chains, and enhancing the resilience of supply chains that rely on the Panama Canal, the US can reduce its dependence on foreign adversaries, enhance its economic and national security, and ensure the long-term sustainability of its economy. This will require a coordinated effort across government, industry, and academia to address the challenges and opportunities associated with reshoring and strengthening domestic supply chains.

Addressing trade imbalances with China and promoting fair trade practices are critical for maintaining a level playing field for US businesses and ensuring a healthy global trading system. China's trade practices, including intellectual property theft, forced technology transfer, and the subsidization of state-owned enterprises, have created significant challenges for US businesses, undermining their competitiveness and hindering economic growth.

Intellectual property theft, including cyber espionage and the misappropriation of trade secrets, has become a major concern. Chinese entities, including state-sponsored actors, have engaged in systematic efforts to steal intellectual property from US companies, giving Chinese companies an unfair advantage. Forced technology transfer, where US companies are pressured to share their technology with Chinese partners as a condition for market access, also undermines US innovation and competitiveness.

Furthermore, China's extensive use of subsidies to support state-owned enterprises creates an uneven playing field for US businesses. These subsidies allow Chinese companies to artificially lower prices, undersell US competitors, and gain market share unfairly.

To address these challenges, the US must take a multifaceted approach. Aggressively enforcing existing trade agreements with China and pursuing new agreements that address China's unfair trade practices is crucial. This includes addressing issues such as intellectual property theft, forced technology transfer, market access barriers, and the subsidization of state-owned enterprises.

Imposing tariffs and other trade restrictions on Chinese imports can help to level the playing field and protect US industries from unfair competition. However, it is important to carefully consider the potential impact of such measures on US consumers and the global economy.

Diversifying trade relationships is essential to reduce over-reliance on trade with China. This involves expanding trade with other countries, including countries in Southeast Asia, India, and Latin America, creating new markets for US exports and reducing dependence on the Chinese market.

Supporting domestic industries through measures such as tax incentives, research and development funding, and investment in critical technologies is crucial to enhancing their competitiveness. This will enable US businesses to compete more effectively with Chinese companies and maintain a strong manufacturing base in the United States.

Strengthening international cooperation with allies and partners to address China's unfair trade practices is also vital. Working together through multilateral forums and coordinated actions can increase pressure on China to abide by international trade rules and create a more level playing field for all countries.

By implementing these strategies, the US can promote fair trade practices, address trade imbalances with China, and ensure that US businesses can compete fairly in the global marketplace. This will be essential for maintaining US economic prosperity and ensuring a healthy and balanced global trading system.

Elon Musk's companies, particularly Tesla, can play a significant role in reshoring manufacturing and building more resilient supply chains for the United States. Tesla's experience in China, specifically with the establishment and operation of its Gigafactory Shanghai, provides valuable insights into the challenges and opportunities of manufacturing electric vehicles on a large scale. This experience can be leveraged to inform strategies for expanding domestic manufacturing capabilities in the US, addressing potential challenges, and optimizing production processes for efficiency and cost-effectiveness.

Furthermore, Tesla's focus on vertical integration, controlling key aspects of the production process such as battery manufacturing, can serve as a model for other US companies seeking to reduce reliance on foreign suppliers and enhance their supply chain resilience. By vertically integrating key components of their production process, companies can reduce their vulnerability to supply chain disruptions and ensure a more secure and reliable source of critical components.

SpaceX, with its advancements in rocket technology and launch capabilities, can also contribute to the development of more resilient and efficient supply chains. SpaceX's reusable rockets and efficient launch systems can significantly reduce the cost and time required to transport goods globally, enabling faster and more reliable delivery of goods and materials. This can enhance the agility and responsiveness of global supply chains, mitigating the risks associated with disruptions and geopolitical instability.

By investing in domestic manufacturing, expanding its US operations, and leveraging its technological expertise, Tesla can contribute to the reshoring of critical industries and the strengthening of US supply chains. This can help to reduce reliance on foreign suppliers, particularly in China, enhance national security, and boost US economic competitiveness. However, it's important to note that the role of Tesla and other companies in reshoring manufacturing will depend on various factors, including government policies, market demand, the availability of skilled labor, and the availability of critical resources within the US.

Chapter 6 – Forging Stronger Alliances

Deepening ties with allies and partners in the Indo-Pacific region, particularly those in Southeast Asia such as the Philippines, Indonesia, Vietnam, and others, is crucial for maintaining US influence and countering China's growing assertiveness. Strengthening these relationships requires a multifaceted approach that encompasses security, economic, and diplomatic cooperation.

Enhancing military cooperation is paramount. This includes conducting joint military exercises, increasing intelligence sharing, and providing defense equipment and training to regional partners. Strengthening existing alliances like the US-Philippines Mutual Defense Treaty and forging new partnerships with key regional players are crucial to enhancing collective security and deterring potential aggression.

Deepening economic ties is equally important. Expanding trade and investment ties with regional partners, promoting regional economic integration, and supporting regional infrastructure development initiatives can strengthen economic interdependence and foster shared prosperity. This can involve negotiating new trade agreements that address the concerns of regional partners, supporting private sector investment in the region, and promoting regional connectivity through initiatives like the Indo-Pacific Economic Framework (IPEF).

Promoting democratic values and human rights is another key dimension of deepening ties with regional partners. Supporting democratic institutions, promoting human rights, and fostering civil society development in partner countries strengthens regional resilience and promotes long-term stability. This can involve providing diplomatic and financial support to democratic institutions, promoting human rights dialogue, and supporting civil society organizations that advocate for democratic values and human rights.

Countering Chinese influence operations is also crucial. This may involve coordinated efforts with regional partners to address challenges such as Chinese maritime claims in the South China Sea, counter Chinese influence operations in key sectors like telecommunications, and promote a rules-based international order in the region. This can include joint diplomatic initiatives, information sharing, and coordinated responses to Chinese activities that challenge regional stability.

By deepening ties with allies and partners in the Indo-Pacific region through a multifaceted approach that encompasses security, economic, and diplomatic cooperation, the US can strengthen its regional presence, counter China's growing influence, and promote a stable and prosperous region based on shared values and mutual interests. This will be crucial for maintaining US leadership in the Indo-Pacific and ensuring the long-term security and prosperity of the region.

Countering Chinese influence in emerging markets and building a global coalition to address shared challenges are critical aspects of US foreign policy in the face of China's growing global power. China's expanding economic and political influence in emerging markets presents both opportunities and challenges for the United States. While engagement with China is necessary, it is crucial to counter its efforts to undermine US interests and promote a rules-based international order.

Countering Chinese influence in emerging markets requires a multifaceted approach. This includes offering alternative development models to China's Belt and Road Initiative (BRI).

The BRI, while promoting infrastructure development, has raised concerns about debt traps, environmental degradation, and the erosion of local sovereignty. The US can offer alternative development models that emphasize transparency, sustainability, respect for sovereignty, and adherence to international norms and standards. This could involve supporting initiatives that promote regional integration and connectivity while upholding democratic values, environmental standards, and human rights.

Addressing concerns about Chinese investment practices is also crucial. This includes working with partner countries to address concerns about predatory lending practices, debt traps, and the potential for Chinese investment to undermine local sovereignty and environmental standards.

Countering Chinese influence operations is another critical aspect. China employs a range of tactics to shape global perceptions and influence public opinion, including propaganda campaigns, disinformation operations, and the use of state-sponsored media outlets. Countering these efforts requires strengthening public diplomacy efforts, supporting independent media, and promoting critical thinking and media literacy to help citizens and policymakers discern accurate information and resist manipulative narratives.

Building a global coalition to address shared challenges is essential to effectively counter China's influence and address global issues such as climate change, pandemics, and terrorism. This involves strengthening existing alliances and partnerships with key allies and partners, such as those within the G7, NATO, and the Quad (US, India, Japan, and Australia).

Furthermore, forging new partnerships with emerging powers and developing countries is crucial to building a broader coalition of like-minded nations. This can involve engaging with countries in Africa, Latin America, and Southeast Asia to address shared challenges and promote a rules-based international order.

Reinvigorating international institutions such as the United Nations, the World Bank, and the International Monetary Fund is also essential. These institutions play a vital role in addressing global challenges, promoting cooperation among nations, and upholding international law.

By countering Chinese influence in emerging markets and building a global coalition to address shared challenges, the US can promote its values and interests, uphold the rules-based international order, and ensure a more stable and prosperous world for all. This will require a sustained and coordinated effort across all dimensions of US foreign policy, including diplomacy, economic engagement, and security cooperation.

Strengthening alliances with countries that have strategic interests in the security of the Panama Canal is crucial for maintaining the free flow of global trade and ensuring regional stability. The Panama Canal is a vital waterway for global commerce, connecting the Atlantic and Pacific Oceans and facilitating trade between North and South America, Asia, and Europe.

The security of the Panama Canal is essential for global trade and economic prosperity. Any disruption to the canal's operations, whether through natural disasters such as earthquakes or hurricanes, human-caused incidents such as accidents or acts of sabotage, or geopolitical instability in the region, could have significant economic and geopolitical consequences. A disruption to canal operations could lead to severe disruptions in global supply chains, causing shortages of essential goods, increasing transportation costs, and potentially triggering economic crises.

Strengthening alliances with countries that have strategic interests in the security of the Panama Canal involves a multifaceted approach. Enhancing military cooperation and intelligence sharing with key regional partners, including the United States, is crucial. This includes joint military exercises, intelligence sharing, and the provision of security assistance to ensure the protection of the canal and surrounding areas.

Promoting regional stability is also critical for ensuring the continued operation of the Panama Canal. This involves working with regional partners to address security challenges in the region, such as transnational crime, drug trafficking, and terrorism, that could potentially disrupt the operation of the canal. Addressing these security challenges requires a coordinated regional effort to enhance maritime security, counter illicit activities, and promote peace and stability within the region.

Fostering economic growth and development in the region is also essential for enhancing the security of the Panama Canal.

Economic development can contribute to regional stability by reducing poverty, inequality, and social unrest, which can be significant drivers of conflict. Supporting regional economic integration and promoting sustainable development initiatives can contribute to a more stable and prosperous region, thereby reducing the risks to the security of the Panama Canal.

By strengthening alliances with countries that have strategic interests in the security of the Panama Canal, enhancing regional security cooperation, promoting economic development, and addressing regional challenges, the international community can ensure the continued free flow of trade, promote regional stability, and safeguard this vital waterway for the benefit of the global economy.

SpaceX, through its technological advancements and innovative approaches to space exploration, can significantly contribute to US diplomacy and international cooperation. SpaceX's reusable rockets and advanced launch capabilities have revolutionized space transportation, reducing the cost of access to space and enabling more frequent and affordable space missions. This not only enhances US military and strategic capabilities but also provides opportunities for strengthening alliances with key partners in areas such as space exploration and defense.

By offering its launch services to other countries, SpaceX can facilitate international cooperation in space exploration. This can involve launching satellites for other nations, participating in international space projects, and collaborating with other countries on space exploration initiatives. Such collaborations can foster trust and understanding among nations, promote peaceful and sustainable space exploration, and advance the common good.

SpaceX's Starlink satellite internet constellation has the potential to significantly impact global communication and cooperation. By providing high-speed internet access to remote and underserved communities around the world, Starlink can bridge the digital divide, enhance communication and cooperation between nations, and facilitate disaster relief efforts. This can have a profound impact on economic development, social progress, and international cooperation in addressing global challenges.

Furthermore, SpaceX's technological achievements serve as a powerful symbol of American innovation and technological leadership, inspiring other countries and fostering international cooperation in the field of space exploration. SpaceX's success can encourage other nations to invest in their own space programs, leading to increased international collaboration and a shared commitment to peaceful space exploration.

By leveraging its technological advancements and pursuing a collaborative approach to space exploration, SpaceX can contribute significantly to US diplomacy and international cooperation. This can strengthen alliances, promote global connectivity, and advance the cause of peaceful and sustainable space exploration, ultimately contributing to a more interconnected and prosperous world.

Chapter 7 – Countering Aggression and Promoting Freedom

Developing and implementing a robust deterrence strategy to counter Chinese aggression in the Indo-Pacific, including in the South China Sea and around Taiwan, is a critical national security objective for the United States. China's growing assertiveness in the region, including its military expansion, assertive territorial claims, and efforts to undermine the rules-based international order, poses significant challenges to US interests and regional stability.

A robust deterrence strategy requires a multifaceted approach that combines diplomatic, economic, and military measures. Strengthening alliances and partnerships with key allies and partners in the Indo-Pacific, such as Japan, Australia, India, and the Philippines, is paramount. This includes conducting joint military exercises, enhancing intelligence sharing, and providing defense equipment and training to strengthen collective security capabilities.

Modernizing military capabilities is crucial to maintain a credible military presence in the region. This involves investing in advanced military capabilities, including aircraft carriers, submarines, long-range bombers, and advanced missile systems, to ensure that the US military can effectively deter potential aggression and respond to any contingencies.

Maintaining a technological edge is also critical. Investing in critical technologies such as artificial intelligence, 5G, and semiconductors is crucial to maintaining US technological leadership and countering China's economic and technological influence. This will ensure that the US can maintaining a competitive advantage in key sectors and address the challenges posed by China's technological advancements.

Diplomatic engagement and dialogue are essential while firmly upholding US interests and international rules and norms. This includes maintaining open lines of communication with China to address areas of disagreement, explore areas of potential cooperation, and prevent miscalculations that could lead to conflict. However, this engagement must be coupled with a firm and unwavering commitment to upholding international law and defending the interests of the US and its allies.

Countering Chinese influence operations is also crucial. China employs a range of tactics to undermine US influence and sow discord among allies, including propaganda campaigns, disinformation operations, and efforts to interfere in domestic political processes. Countering these efforts requires strengthening public diplomacy, supporting independent media, and promoting critical thinking and media literacy to help citizens and policymakers identify and counter Chinese influence operations.

Supporting regional stability and prosperity is another key element of a robust deterrence strategy. This includes promoting economic development, supporting democratic institutions, and addressing regional challenges such as climate change and maritime security. A stable and prosperous region is less likely to be susceptible to instability and conflict, which could have significant security implications for the United States.

By implementing these strategies, the US can deter Chinese aggression, maintain peace and stability in the Indo-Pacific, and uphold the rules-based international order. This will require a sustained and coordinated effort across all dimensions of US foreign policy, including diplomacy, military power, economic engagement, and information operations.

Supporting democracy and human rights in Hong Kong and Taiwan is a critical element of US foreign policy and a cornerstone of its commitment to upholding the rules-based international order. The erosion of freedoms and autonomy in Hong Kong under the National Security Law is a grave concern. The implementation of this law has led to the suppression of dissent, the erosion of judicial independence, and the shrinking of civic space, undermining the "one country, two systems" framework that was intended to guarantee Hong Kong's freedoms and autonomy.

The US must continue to support the people of Hong Kong in their fight for democracy, freedom, and the rule of law. This includes imposing targeted sanctions on individuals and entities responsible for human rights abuses in Hong Kong, such as those involved in the suppression of dissent, the erosion of judicial independence, and the abduction of Hong Kong residents. Providing safe haven and support for Hong Kong residents fleeing persecution, including those seeking asylum in the United States, is also crucial. Furthermore, the US must continue to speak out forcefully against the erosion of freedoms and the suppression of dissent in Hong Kong, using diplomatic channels and public statements to express its deep concerns and call for the restoration of freedoms and the rule of law.

With regard to Taiwan, the US must continue to uphold its commitment to the Taiwan Relations Act, which provides for the sale of defensive weapons to Taiwan and opposes any unilateral changes to the status quo across the Taiwan Strait. This includes strengthening security cooperation with Taiwan, deepening economic ties, and actively opposing any attempts by China to coerce or intimidate Taiwan. The US must also make it clear that any attempt by China to use force to reunify with Taiwan would have serious consequences.

By supporting democracy and human rights in Hong Kong and Taiwan, the US can demonstrate its commitment to these values and uphold the rules-based international order in the face of growing authoritarianism. This will not only benefit the people of Hong Kong and Taiwan but also serve as a powerful signal to other countries that the US stands with those who advocate for democracy, human rights, and the rule of law.

Countering Chinese influence operations and cyberattacks is a critical national security priority for the United States. China has increasingly employed a range of tactics to undermine US influence, sow discord among allies, and steal sensitive information, posing significant challenges to US national security and economic competitiveness.

Chinese influence operations encompass a wide range of activities, including propaganda campaigns, disinformation operations, and efforts to infiltrate US institutions and manipulate public opinion. These operations aim to undermine public trust in US institutions, sow discord among allies, and advance China's political and strategic objectives.

Countering these influence operations requires a multifaceted approach. Strengthening public diplomacy efforts is crucial to counter Chinese propaganda and disinformation campaigns. This includes promoting accurate information, supporting independent media, and fostering critical thinking and media literacy among the public to help them discern accurate information and resist manipulative narratives.

Protecting US elections from foreign interference, including cyberattacks and disinformation campaigns aimed at influencing public opinion and election outcomes, is paramount. This requires strengthening election security measures, investigating and disrupting foreign interference operations, and holding accountable those responsible for such activities.

Addressing the threat of foreign malign influence on US institutions is also critical. This includes identifying and countering Chinese influence operations aimed at infiltrating US government agencies, academic institutions, and critical infrastructure.

Countering Chinese cyberattacks is equally crucial. China has significantly increased its cyber capabilities, posing a significant threat to US critical infrastructure, government systems, and private sector networks.

Improving cybersecurity measures to protect critical infrastructure and sensitive data from cyberattacks originating from China is paramount. This includes investing in advanced cybersecurity technologies, improving cybersecurity training and awareness, and strengthening international cooperation to combat cyber threats.

Developing and deploying advanced cyber defense capabilities, such as artificial intelligence and machine learning-powered threat detection systems, is crucial to effectively counter sophisticated cyberattacks.

Strengthening international cooperation with allies and partners to share intelligence, develop best practices, and coordinate responses to cyber threats is also essential.

By implementing these strategies, the US can effectively counter Chinese influence operations and cyberattacks, protect its national security interests, and maintain its leadership in the global arena. This will require a sustained and coordinated effort across government agencies, the private sector, and academia to address the evolving cyber threat landscape and ensure the security and resilience of critical systems and infrastructure.

The Philippines faces a complex security environment in the Indo-Pacific region, characterized by territorial disputes in the South China Sea, the threat of terrorism, and the increasing impact of natural disasters. Strengthening the Philippines' defense capabilities is crucial to ensure its ability to defend its sovereignty, protect its territorial integrity, and respond effectively to these challenges.

Increasing military presence and cooperation with allies, particularly the United States, is essential to enhance Philippine defense capabilities. Enhanced military cooperation can significantly bolster the Philippines' ability to address these security challenges. This includes conducting regular joint military exercises, such as maritime patrols, counterterrorism operations, and humanitarian assistance and disaster relief operations. These exercises enhance interoperability, improve combat readiness, and strengthen the bonds between the two militaries, fostering trust and mutual understanding.

Providing the Philippines with access to advanced military equipment, such as aircraft, ships, and surveillance systems, is also critical. This includes not only the provision of equipment but also the provision of training and maintenance support to ensure the effective and sustainable use of these systems.

Enhancing intelligence sharing and information exchange between the US and Philippine militaries is crucial to improving situational awareness, countering threats, and enhancing maritime domain awareness. This includes sharing intelligence on potential threats, coordinating maritime patrols, and collaborating on counterterrorism efforts.

Increased US military presence in the Philippines, such as through the rotational deployment of US forces, can also serve as a deterrent to potential aggression and provide a tangible demonstration of US commitment to the defense of the

Philippines. This can include the increased presence of US naval and air forces in the region, as well as the rotation of US military personnel through Philippine military bases.

By increasing military presence and cooperation with allies in the Philippines, the US can significantly enhance the Philippines' defense capabilities, strengthen regional security, and contribute to the maintenance of peace and stability in the Indo-Pacific region. This will be crucial for countering emerging security challenges, protecting US interests, and upholding the rules-based international order in the face of growing regional competition.

The Panama Canal stands as a crucial artery for global trade, its strategic significance for the United States undeniable. However, the growing Chinese influence in the region casts a shadow of concern, raising legitimate questions about the Canal's continued security and unimpeded operation. To effectively address these potential threats, a multifaceted approach is necessary, necessitating the development of comprehensive contingency plans.

Strengthening partnerships is paramount. Deepening cooperation with Panama is essential to ensure the Canal's continued independent operation and safeguard its security. Furthermore, enhancing security and intelligence sharing with regional partners in Latin America will bolster collective capabilities and improve situational awareness.

Diversifying trade routes is another critical element. Exploring alternative shipping routes, such as the Arctic routes or expanding the utilization of the Suez Canal, can mitigate reliance on the Panama Canal and reduce vulnerability to potential disruptions. Simultaneously, supporting infrastructure development across the Americas will enhance regional connectivity, creating alternative trade flows and lessening the dependence on a single chokepoint.

Investing in alternative technologies offers a promising avenue. Exploring and investing in innovative technologies, such as advancements in shipbuilding and cargo transportation, has the potential to diminish the strategic importance of the Panama Canal.

Proactively addressing Chinese influence is crucial. Countering Chinese economic and political influence in the region requires a multifaceted approach, encompassing diplomatic engagement, the provision of economic incentives, and the initiation of infrastructure development initiatives. Moreover, meticulous monitoring of Chinese investment in infrastructure projects near the Canal is imperative to assess potential security implications and proactively mitigate any risks.

It is important to emphasize that these are merely a few potential measures. A more in-depth analysis is required to develop specific and effective contingency plans that can safeguard the security and continued operation of the Panama Canal in the face of evolving geopolitical realities.

Elon Musk's companies, particularly SpaceX and Starlink, possess the potential to significantly enhance US military capabilities and bolster national security in several key ways. Starlink, a constellation of low-Earth orbit satellites, provides high-speed, low-latency internet access globally. This capability is invaluable for the military, enabling reliable and secure communication links for troops on the ground, even in remote or contested areas. It also facilitates improved situational awareness through real-time data transmission from drones, sensors, and other platforms, allowing for faster decision-making and more effective targeting. Furthermore, Starlink enables increased intelligence gathering by facilitating the collection and dissemination of intelligence data from various sources.

SpaceX, with its reusable rockets like Falcon 9 and Starship, has revolutionized space access. Reduced launch costs make space operations more affordable and enable more frequent missions. Increased launch flexibility allows for rapid responses to emerging threats and the ability to deploy assets on demand. This significantly enhances military space capabilities by facilitating the deployment and maintenance of military satellites for communications, surveillance, and other critical functions.

The development of Starship, a powerful and reusable launch vehicle, also paves the way for hypersonic technologies. These technologies could potentially be leveraged for rapid global strike capabilities, enabling the delivery of payloads with unprecedented speed and accuracy. Additionally, they could contribute to the development of advanced missile defense systems, providing the ability to intercept and neutralize ballistic missiles.

It's important to acknowledge that the integration of these technologies into the US military presents both benefits and potential challenges. Over-reliance on SpaceX technologies could create vulnerabilities if disruptions occur. Ensuring the security and resilience of Starlink and other SpaceX systems against cyberattacks is critical. Furthermore, the potential use of these technologies for offensive or controversial purposes must be carefully considered and regulated.

Overall, Elon Musk's technologies offer significant potential to enhance US military capabilities and bolster national security. However, careful planning, responsible integration, and a thorough assessment of potential risks are crucial to ensure these technologies are used effectively and ethically.

The integration of Elon Musk's technologies into US military and intelligence operations presents a complex landscape of ethical and security implications. The potential for increased automation in warfare, particularly with the development of hypersonic technologies, raises concerns about the erosion of human control in decision-making processes. Questions arise regarding the ethical implications of autonomous weapons systems and the potential for unintended consequences or escalation of conflict.

The use of technologies like Starlink for surveillance and targeting raises concerns about the potential for disproportionate harm to civilians and the risk of discrimination in the application of force. The use of private sector technologies in military operations raises questions about accountability and transparency. Determining responsibility for actions taken using these technologies and ensuring appropriate oversight mechanisms are in place are crucial. Many of these technologies have both civilian and military applications. This dual-use nature presents challenges in regulating their development and deployment, ensuring they are not misused or proliferated to adversaries.

Integrating private sector technologies into critical military systems increases the attack surface for adversaries. Cyberattacks targeting SpaceX infrastructure or Starlink could disrupt military communications, surveillance, and even command and control systems. Over-reliance on SpaceX technologies could create vulnerabilities if disruptions occur due to company failures, supply chain disruptions, or even government intervention. The collection and use of vast amounts of data by Starlink for military purposes raise significant privacy concerns. Robust safeguards are needed to protect sensitive information and ensure compliance with relevant laws and regulations. The widespread availability of advanced technologies like those developed by SpaceX could potentially accelerate the arms race and increase the risk of their proliferation to other actors, including non-state actors.

Addressing these ethical and security implications requires careful consideration, open dialogue, and the development of appropriate safeguards and regulations. This includes establishing clear ethical guidelines for the use of these technologies in military operations, strengthening cybersecurity measures, and fostering transparency and accountability in their development and deployment.

## Part 3 – Implementing the Winning Strategy

Successfully implementing any winning strategy requires a robust and responsive government. In Part 3, 'Implementing the Winning Strategy,' and specifically Chapter 8, 'Reforming Government and Mobilizing Resources,' we confront the challenges of modernizing our government institutions, streamlining processes, and ensuring the efficient allocation of resources to achieve our shared goals.

## Chapter 8 – Reforming Government and Mobilizing Resources

Investing in long-term strategic priorities and streamlining government bureaucracy are critical for effective governance in the 21st century. A focus on short-term political cycles often hinders the ability of governments to make informed decisions that align with national interests and foster sustainable development. By prioritizing long-term goals, governments can invest in critical areas such as infrastructure development, education, research and development, and environmental protection, ensuring a more prosperous and sustainable future for their citizens. This necessitates a shift in mindset, moving away from reactive policies driven by immediate electoral considerations and embracing a commitment to long-term planning and execution.

Furthermore, excessive bureaucracy within government can significantly impede decision-making and hinder the efficient allocation of resources. Complex and redundant procedures, layers of approval, and a lack of clear lines of accountability can lead to delays, inefficiencies, and ultimately, a misallocation of public funds. Streamlining government bureaucracy is essential to address these challenges. By simplifying proccsscs, eliminating unnecessary red tape, and empowering frontline workers with the authority and resources to make timely decisions, governments can enhance their responsiveness to citizens' needs and ensure that public resources are used effectively and efficiently to achieve desired outcomes.

These two interconnected strategies – investing in long-term strategic priorities and streamlining government bureaucracy – are not mutually exclusive but rather complementary. By prioritizing long-term goals and simultaneously streamlining government operations, governments can create a more agile, responsive, and effective system that is better equipped to address the complex challenges of the 21st century, from climate change and economic inequality to technological advancements and demographic shifts.

Fostering a sense of national unity and purpose is paramount for mobilizing public support for the long-term competition with China. This necessitates a clear and compelling narrative that articulates the stakes of this competition for the American people. It is crucial to emphasize the shared values and interests that unite the nation, transcending political divisions and fostering a sense of common purpose.

Open and honest communication with the public about the challenges posed by China is essential. This involves transparently discussing the economic, technological, and geopolitical implications of China's rise while simultaneously highlighting the opportunities for the United States to maintain its competitive edge and ensure a prosperous future for all Americans.

Furthermore, emphasizing shared American values such as democracy, freedom, and innovation can serve as a powerful unifying force. By framing the competition with China as a defense of these core values and a reaffirmation of American exceptionalism, it is possible to garner broader public support for the necessary investments in research and development, infrastructure, and education.

Building a strong sense of national unity also requires addressing the concerns and anxieties of different segments of the population. Ensuring that the benefits of economic growth and technological advancement are shared broadly is crucial. All Americans must have the opportunity to participate in and contribute to the nation's success. By fostering a sense of shared purpose and ensuring that all Americans feel invested in the nation's future, the United States can effectively mobilize the necessary resources and support to compete successfully with China in the 21st century.

Government-industry partnerships are crucial drivers of innovation and economic growth. By fostering collaboration between the public and private sectors, governments can leverage the unique strengths of each to address complex challenges and accelerate technological advancements. This dynamic becomes particularly impactful when working with cutting-edge companies like SpaceX and Tesla, which push the boundaries of innovation in their respective fields.

SpaceX provides a prime example of how this synergy can revolutionize an industry. Government funding through agencies like NASA has been instrumental in supporting SpaceX's development of reusable rockets, a technological feat that has significantly reduced launch costs and opened up new possibilities for space exploration. This partnership not only benefits the space industry itself but also has broader economic implications, fostering job creation and driving technological advancements with applications far beyond space travel, such as advancements in materials science, robotics, and artificial intelligence.

Similarly, Tesla's advancements in electric vehicle technology exemplify the power of this collaborative model. Government incentives such as tax credits and subsidies have encouraged the adoption of electric vehicles, while Tesla's pioneering work in battery technology and vehicle design has pushed the boundaries of what is possible in the automotive industry. This collaboration has not only accelerated the transition to electric vehicles but has also spurred innovation in other sectors, such as renewable energy, energy storage, and autonomous driving technologies.

These examples demonstrate the significant potential of government-industry partnerships to drive innovation and economic growth. By fostering collaboration, supporting research and development, and creating an enabling environment for innovation, governments can unlock the full potential of cutting-edge companies and position themselves at the forefront of technological advancement. However, careful consideration must be given to the terms of these partnerships, ensuring that they are mutually beneficial and that public interests, such as environmental protection, consumer safety, and national security, are adequately protected.

Chapter 9 – Winning the Information War

Counteracting Chinese propaganda and disinformation campaigns effectively requires a multifaceted approach. Strengthening media literacy within populations is crucial. This involves educating individuals on how to critically evaluate information, identify potential biases, recognize common propaganda techniques such as misinformation, disinformation, and manipulation, and understand the sources and motivations behind information.

Investing in independent media is essential to counter the influence of state-sponsored propaganda. Supporting independent journalism and research institutions strengthens the ability to produce accurate and reliable information, providing a crucial counterweight to narratives disseminated by state-controlled media outlets.

Leveraging technology is vital in the fight against disinformation. Developing and utilizing AI-powered tools to identify and flag potentially misleading information, track the spread of disinformation campaigns, and analyze the tactics employed by foreign actors are crucial for effective countermeasures.

International cooperation is necessary to effectively combat global disinformation campaigns. Sharing information and best practices among countries facing similar challenges can enhance collective efforts, improve response times, and develop more effective countermeasures.

Finally, proactive communication and engagement with the public are crucial. Governments and credible sources need to proactively communicate accurate information and address public concerns effectively. This includes countering the narratives promoted by disinformation campaigns with clear and concise messaging that resonates with the public and provides accurate information about global events and geopolitical realities.

Leveraging technology to advance American values and narratives globally presents both a significant opportunity and a complex challenge. Technology offers powerful tools for communication, information dissemination, and cultural exchange, enabling the United States to effectively promote its values such as democracy, freedom, human rights, and individual liberty.

This can be achieved through various means. Supporting and promoting independent media outlets and platforms that provide diverse perspectives and counter harmful narratives is crucial. Furthermore, developing and deploying innovative technologies that enhance global connectivity and access to information, such as high-speed internet infrastructure and digital literacy programs, can empower individuals and promote the free flow of information. Utilizing social media and other digital platforms to engage with global audiences, share authentic American stories, and foster cultural exchange can also effectively advance American values and narratives.

However, it is crucial to acknowledge the potential pitfalls. The use of technology for influence operations can be easily misused and may have unintended consequences. It is essential to ensure that any such efforts are conducted ethically, transparently, and with respect for the sovereignty and cultural sensitivities of other nations.

Furthermore, it is crucial to recognize that technological advancements can also be used by adversaries to spread disinformation, manipulate public opinion, and undermine democratic values. Therefore, a robust and proactive approach is necessary, one that not only leverages technology to advance American values but also mitigates the risks associated with its use. This requires a comprehensive strategy that includes developing and implementing safeguards against cyberattacks, combating disinformation campaigns, and promoting responsible and ethical use of technology in the international arena.

Strengthening international media freedom and supporting independent journalism are fundamental to a healthy democracy and an informed citizenry. A free and independent media plays a vital role in holding governments and powerful actors accountable, providing diverse perspectives, fostering informed public discourse, and ultimately empowering citizens to make informed decisions.

Ensuring the safety of journalists is paramount. Governments must unequivocally condemn attacks on journalists and hold perpetrators accountable. This includes protecting journalists from harassment, intimidation, and violence, both online and offline.

Combating censorship and restrictions on press freedom is essential. This involves advocating for the repeal of laws that restrict press freedom, such as those that criminalize defamation or limit access to information. Governments must uphold the right to freedom of expression and ensure that journalists can operate without fear of reprisal.

Promoting media pluralism and diversity is crucial to prevent the dominance of a single narrative and ensure a plurality of voices. Supporting a diverse media landscape, including independent outlets, local news sources, and citizen journalism, fosters a more informed and engaged public.

Addressing the economic challenges faced by independent media is vital for their long-term sustainability. Supporting sustainable business models for independent journalism, such as through public media funding, tax incentives, or innovative subscription models, is essential to ensure their continued viability and independence.

Fostering international cooperation among governments, media organizations, and civil society is crucial to addressing global threats to media freedom, such as disinformation and cyberattacks. Sharing best practices, coordinating responses to threats, and advocating for international standards of media freedom are essential for creating a global environment where independent journalism can thrive.

By strengthening international media freedom and supporting independent journalism, we can ensure a more informed, engaged, and democratic society where citizens have access to accurate and reliable information, are empowered to participate in public discourse, and can hold their leaders accountable.

Social media platforms and other communication technologies play a profound role in shaping public discourse and influencing public opinion in the US-China competition. These platforms serve as powerful tools for both information dissemination and manipulation.

Both the US and China utilize social media to project their narratives, influence public opinion, and mobilize support for their respective positions. This includes disseminating information about their economic, political, and military advancements while simultaneously attempting to discredit their rival.

However, these platforms are also susceptible to exploitation. Foreign actors, including state-sponsored entities, can utilize social media to spread disinformation, manipulate public opinion, and sow discord within target societies. This can include the dissemination of false or misleading information, the amplification of extremist voices, and the targeting of specific demographics with tailored propaganda.

Furthermore, the algorithms that govern these platforms can inadvertently amplify extremist views, create echo chambers, and limit exposure to diverse perspectives. This can contribute to the polarization of public opinion and make it more difficult to engage in constructive dialogue and find common ground.

The use of communication technologies in the US-China competition presents both opportunities and challenges. While these technologies can be powerful tools for promoting understanding and fostering cooperation, they also pose significant risks, including the spread of disinformation, the manipulation of public opinion, and the exacerbation of existing societal divisions.

It is crucial to develop strategies for mitigating these risks, such as promoting media literacy, supporting independent journalism, and enhancing the transparency and accountability of social media platforms. By understanding the complexities of this issue, policymakers and the public can harness the power of communication technologies to promote constructive dialogue and foster a more informed and engaged citizenry.

Elon Musk's acquisition of Twitter has profound implications for the information landscape and significantly impacts the US-China competition. Twitter serves as a crucial platform for the dissemination of news, the exchange of ideas, and the mobilization of public opinion, shaping global discourse and influencing policy debates.

Since Musk's takeover, significant changes in content moderation policies have been observed. Some users have experienced increased visibility, while others face restrictions, raising concerns about the platform's role in shaping public discourse and the potential for the spread of misinformation and manipulation.

In the context of the US-China competition, Twitter plays a pivotal role. Both countries utilize the platform to disseminate their narratives, influence public opinion, and engage in information warfare. Musk's ownership has the potential to significantly alter this dynamic. Changes to content moderation policies could impact the ability of US government agencies and independent media to effectively counter Chinese disinformation campaigns while simultaneously creating potential opportunities for Chinese actors to exploit the platform for their own propaganda purposes.

Furthermore, Musk's acquisition has raised concerns about potential biases in content moderation and the platform's susceptibility to being used to further specific political agendas. These concerns have broader implications for the integrity of public discourse and the information ecosystem, crucial factors in the US-China competition.

The long-term impact of Musk's ownership on Twitter remains uncertain. However, the platform's evolution under his leadership will undoubtedly have significant consequences for the information landscape and its role in the ongoing US-China competition.

Chapter 10 – Securing America's Future

Investing in education and workforce development is paramount for the United States to maintain a competitive advantage in the global economy. A highly skilled and adaptable workforce is essential to drive innovation, increase productivity, and ensure long-term economic growth.

This requires a multifaceted approach that addresses the needs of individuals at all stages of their education and career journeys.

Firstly, investing in early childhood education is crucial. High-quality early childhood education programs provide a strong foundation for future learning and development, ensuring that all children have the opportunity to reach their full potential.

Secondly, improving K-12 education is essential. This includes strengthening STEM education, increasing access to quality teachers and resources, and addressing inequities in educational opportunities across different communities.

Thirdly, expanding access to affordable and high-quality higher education is critical. This includes increasing access to financial aid, reducing student loan debt, and ensuring that higher education institutions are adequately funded to meet the demands of the 21st-century workforce.

Furthermore, investing in workforce development programs is essential to equip individuals with the skills and knowledge they need to succeed in the modern economy. This includes supporting programs that provide job training, apprenticeships, and reskilling opportunities for displaced workers.

Finally, fostering strong partnerships between education providers, businesses, and government is crucial to ensure that education and training programs align with the needs of the labor market. These partnerships can help identify in-demand skills, develop relevant training programs, and create pathways for individuals to transition smoothly from education to employment.

By investing in education and workforce development at all levels, the United States can cultivate a highly skilled and adaptable workforce, drive innovation, and maintain its competitive edge in the global economy.

Maintaining a strong and modern American military is crucial for deterring potential adversaries and ensuring national security in an increasingly complex and uncertain world. This requires a multifaceted approach that prioritizes innovation, readiness, and strategic partnerships.

Investing in cutting-edge technologies is paramount. This includes developing and fielding advanced capabilities in areas such as artificial intelligence, hypersonic weapons, cyber warfare, and space-based systems. Modernizing existing platforms and developing new ones, such as next-generation aircraft and unmanned vehicles, is essential to maintaining technological superiority.

Furthermore, ensuring the readiness of military personnel is critical. This includes providing rigorous training, fostering a culture of innovation and adaptability, and ensuring the well-being of service members and their families.

Building and maintaining strong alliances and partnerships with key allies is also vital. Collaborative efforts in areas such as intelligence sharing, joint military exercises, and technology development enhance collective security and project a united front against potential threats.

Finally, it is crucial to maintain a realistic assessment of threats and allocate resources effectively. This requires a clear understanding of the evolving security landscape and a commitment to prioritizing investments in areas that are most critical to national security.

By investing in innovation, maintaining a well-trained and ready force, and fostering strong alliances, the United States can ensure it possesses a military capable of deterring potential adversaries, protecting its interests, and upholding its commitments to allies around the world.

Promoting American values and global leadership is crucial for rallying international support for the rules-based international order. By championing principles such as democracy, human rights, and the rule of law, the United States can inspire confidence and build trust among allies and partners. This requires a consistent and unwavering commitment to these values both domestically and internationally. Upholding these values domestically strengthens the credibility of American foreign policy and demonstrates a genuine commitment to promoting them globally. Actively promoting these values through diplomatic engagement, foreign assistance programs that support democratic development and human rights protections, and robust support for international institutions that uphold these principles is essential.

American leadership in upholding the rules-based international order demands a steadfast commitment to multilateralism and a willingness to work collaboratively with other nations to address global challenges. This requires active participation in international organizations such as the United Nations and the World Trade Organization and a willingness to engage in constructive dialogue and find common ground with other nations, even when there are disagreements.

Furthermore, the United States can leverage its economic and diplomatic influence to encourage other countries to abide by international norms and uphold the principles of free trade, open markets, and peaceful resolution of disputes. By consistently demonstrating a commitment to these principles and working to resolve global challenges through cooperation and diplomacy, the United States can inspire confidence in its leadership and rally international support for a rules-based international order that benefits all nations.

Cultivating a culture of innovation and entrepreneurship is paramount for fostering the next generation of leaders like Elon Musk. Such an environment nurtures creativity, risk-taking, and a relentless pursuit of ambitious goals.

This requires a multi-pronged approach. Firstly, education systems must emphasize critical thinking, problem-solving, and creative exploration, moving beyond rote memorization to foster a deeper understanding of concepts and encourage independent thought. Secondly, fostering a culture that values experimentation and embraces failure as a learning opportunity is crucial. This requires creating safe spaces for individuals to explore new ideas, take risks, and learn from their mistakes without fear of retribution.

Furthermore, access to resources and mentorship is vital. This includes providing access to funding for startups, mentorship programs that connect aspiring entrepreneurs with experienced leaders, and creating vibrant ecosystems that support innovation and entrepreneurship, such as incubators and accelerators.

Finally, fostering a culture of collaboration and interdisciplinary learning is essential. Encouraging cross-pollination of ideas between different fields and fostering a spirit of collaboration can lead to unexpected breakthroughs and drive innovation forward. By cultivating a culture that values creativity, risk-taking, and a relentless pursuit of ambitious goals, we can inspire and empower the next generation of innovators and entrepreneurs to shape the future.

Elon Musk's companies and their technologies have the potential to profoundly impact the future of the United States and its role in the world.

SpaceX, with its reusable rockets and ambitious plans for Mars colonization, could solidify the United States' position as a leader in space exploration and potentially open new frontiers for human civilization. This could enhance national security, bolster economic competitiveness through space-based technologies, and inspire a new generation of scientists and engineers.

Tesla's advancements in electric vehicles and renewable energy technologies could significantly contribute to the fight against climate change and strengthen US leadership in sustainable energy solutions. This could not only enhance energy security but also position the US as a global leader in the transition to a clean energy economy.

However, the long-term implications also present potential challenges. The rapid development of artificial intelligence, a key focus for many of Musk's ventures, raises ethical and societal questions that need careful consideration. Ensuring responsible development and deployment of AI is crucial to mitigate potential risks and harness its benefits for humanity.

Furthermore, the concentration of technological power in the hands of a few companies, including those founded by Elon Musk, raises concerns about potential market dominance, anti-competitive practices, and the potential for unintended consequences.

Ultimately, the long-term implications of Elon Musk's companies and their technologies will depend on a variety of factors, including government regulation, societal values, and the choices made by the companies themselves. By proactively addressing potential challenges and fostering responsible innovation, the United States can harness the transformative power of these technologies to strengthen its global standing and create a more sustainable and prosperous future.

Conclusion

The American Dream, that enduring beacon of hope and opportunity, is at a crossroads. While our nation boasts a rich history of innovation, resilience, and progress, we face unprecedented challenges that threaten to derail the aspirations of future generations. To reclaim the promise of America, we must embark on a bold and ambitious path forward. This necessitates a renewed commitment to investing in our people. Ensuring access to quality education at all levels, from early childhood to higher education and vocational training, is paramount. Strengthening our workforce through robust skills development programs and meaningful apprenticeships will empower individuals and bolster our economy.

Furthermore, fostering a dynamic economy demands a concerted effort. We must actively promote innovation and entrepreneurship through strategic investments in research and development. Supporting small businesses and fostering a level playing field for all Americans are crucial for economic growth and prosperity. Addressing the growing income inequality gap is not merely a matter of social justice but also a matter of economic stability and national security.

Upholding our democratic values is non-negotiable. Protecting the fundamental right to vote, safeguarding the independence of our judiciary, and ensuring a free and independent press are cornerstones of a thriving democracy. We must actively promote civic engagement and foster a more inclusive and equitable society where every voice is heard and every individual has the opportunity to reach their full potential.

The climate crisis demands immediate and decisive action. Transitioning to a clean energy economy, investing in sustainable infrastructure, and protecting our precious natural resources are not just environmental imperatives but also economic opportunities.

Strengthening our communities is essential for a thriving nation. Investing in affordable housing, improving access to quality healthcare, and addressing the opioid epidemic are critical social and economic priorities. Supporting our veterans and ensuring the well-being of all Americans are fundamental obligations of a grateful nation.

This is not the work of any single individual or political party. It requires a collective effort, a coming together of citizens from all walks of life. We must engage in respectful dialogue, find common ground, and work together to build a brighter future for all Americans.

Now is the time for action. Let us roll up our sleeves, embrace the challenges ahead, and together, reclaim the American Dream.

Reiterating the importance of a comprehensive and sustained effort to counter China's challenge is critical for ensuring the long-term security and prosperity of the United States and its allies.

This requires a multifaceted approach that addresses the economic, technological, military, and diplomatic dimensions of the competition.

Economically, this necessitates strengthening domestic industries, diversifying supply chains, and investing in critical technologies such as semiconductors and artificial intelligence.

Technologically, it requires prioritizing research and development, fostering innovation, and protecting critical infrastructure from cyber threats.

Militarily, it requires maintaining a strong and modern military capable of deterring aggression and defending US interests.

Diplomatically, this necessitates strengthening alliances and partnerships, engaging in constructive dialogue with China on areas of mutual interest, and promoting a rules-based international order.

Furthermore, a sustained effort requires long-term commitment and consistent investment across successive administrations. This necessitates developing and implementing a comprehensive national strategy that outlines clear goals, priorities, and measures of success.

By pursuing a comprehensive and sustained approach, the United States can effectively counter China's challenge, safeguard its interests, and ensure a prosperous and secure future for itself and its allies.

The path to American victory demands more than individual ambition; it necessitates a collective will, a unified nation striving towards shared goals. Political gridlock and the corrosive influence of partisan divisions have become crippling obstacles, hindering progress and undermining our ability to effectively address the multifaceted challenges of the 21st century. The complexities of climate change, economic inequality, and social justice demand a holistic approach that transcends ideological divides. We must break free from the shackles of political infighting, embrace a spirit of national unity, and recognize that our strength lies in our diversity and our collective ability to work together for the common good.

Achieving lasting success requires more than just good intentions; it demands strong political will. This necessitates leaders with the courage to make difficult decisions, prioritize long-term vision over short-term political gains, and champion policies that benefit the nation as a whole. We need leaders who inspire confidence, foster trust, and mobilize the American people to rise to the challenges that lie ahead. Leaders who understand that true leadership involves not just commanding but also listening, learning, and uniting the nation around a shared purpose.

Furthermore, a long-term strategic vision is indispensable. We cannot afford to address challenges in isolation; a comprehensive and integrated approach is paramount. We must acknowledge the interconnectedness of our economic, social, and environmental systems. This requires careful planning, strategic investments, and a commitment to sustainable development that ensures prosperity for generations to come. A vision that prioritizes equity, inclusivity, and the well-being of all Americans, not just a select few.

The American Dream is not a relic of the past; it is a beacon of hope, a testament to the enduring spirit of this nation. However, this dream requires our active participation, our unwavering commitment, and our collective resolve. Let us unite, let us lead, and let us envision a future where the promise of America is realized for all, a future where opportunity and prosperity are not privileges but birthrights for every citizen.

Securing America's future demands a potent combination of visionary leadership, relentless innovation, and strategic partnerships. Strong leadership is paramount, guiding the nation through the complex challenges of the 21st century with a clear vision, decisive action, and an unwavering commitment to long-term goals. This leadership must foster an environment that encourages risk-taking, rewards innovation, and empowers individuals and communities to reach their full potential. It requires leaders who can inspire hope, build bridges across divides, and mobilize the nation to address the challenges that lie ahead.

Innovation is the lifeblood of progress, driving economic growth, creating new industries, and improving the quality of life for all Americans. Investing in research and development, nurturing a culture of creativity, and supporting entrepreneurship are not just economic imperatives; they are essential for maintaining America's competitive edge in a rapidly evolving global landscape. By embracing new technologies, fostering a spirit of discovery, and encouraging out-of-the-box thinking, we can ensure that America remains at the forefront of innovation and continues to shape the future.

Furthermore, forging strategic partnerships is essential in addressing the interconnected challenges of our time. Collaborating with allies, engaging with international organizations, and fostering strong relationships with businesses, academia, and civil society are not just diplomatic niceties; they are vital for tackling issues such as climate change, global health, and economic inequality. These challenges transcend borders, and effective solutions require a global perspective and a collective effort. By working together, we can leverage our strengths, share knowledge and resources, and achieve outcomes that are greater than the sum of their parts.

By embracing these key elements – visionary leadership, relentless innovation, and strategic partnerships – America can navigate the complexities of the 21st century, ensuring a prosperous and secure future for generations to come. A future where opportunity is not just a promise but a reality for all Americans, a future where innovation drives progress, and a future where America continues to lead the world in the pursuit of a better tomorrow.

The path to American victory demands a renewed commitment to its founding principles: liberty, justice, and equality for all. This is not merely a lofty ideal; it is a practical imperative for a thriving and just society. We must invest in our people, ensuring access to quality education at all levels, from early childhood to higher education and vocational training. Affordable healthcare must be a fundamental right, not a privilege, ensuring that all Americans can live healthy and productive lives. Furthermore, we must create an economic system that provides opportunities for all, regardless of background, dismantling systemic barriers that perpetuate inequality and marginalization. We must strive to create a society where every individual, regardless of race, gender, ethnicity, or socioeconomic status, has the chance to reach their full potential and contribute meaningfully to our nation.

Moreover, America must embrace its role as a global leader, not through military might alone but through the power of its ideals. We must champion democracy, human rights, and international cooperation, fostering a foreign policy that prioritizes diplomacy, engages with allies, and addresses global challenges such as climate change, poverty, and conflict. We must invest in sustainable development, promote peace and security, and work towards a world where all people can live in dignity and freedom.

Looking ahead, I envision a United States that leads the world not through coercion, but through inspiration. A nation that fosters innovation, champions a future where opportunity, prosperity, and justice are within reach for all, and embodies the values of liberty, equality, and human dignity. A nation that serves as a beacon of hope, not just for its own citizens, but for people around the globe yearning for a better future. A future where the promise of America is not just a distant dream but a lived reality for all.

www.ingramcontent.com/pod-product-compliance
Ingram Content Group UK Ltd.
Pitfield, Milton Keynes, MK11 3LW, UK
UKHW040742060225
454761UK00001B/12